The Soccer Starter

The Soccer Starter

*Your Guide to
Coaching Young Players*

William C. Summers

ILLUSTRATED BY ROBERT JOHN REEDY

McFarland & Company, Inc., Publishers
Jefferson, North Carolina, and London

LIBRARY OF CONGRESS CATALOGUING-IN-PUBLICATION DATA

Summers, William C., 1959–
    The soccer starter : your guide to coaching young players /
by William C. Summers.
        p.   cm.
    Includes index.

    ISBN 978-0-7864-1187-2
    (softcover : 60# alkaline paper) ∞

    1. Soccer for children—Coaching.   I. Title.
GV943.8.S86   2002
796.334'07'7—dc21   2002004233

British Library cataloguing data are available

Manufactured in the United States of America

McFarland & Company, Inc., Publishers
  Box 611, Jefferson, North Carolina 28640
    www.mcfarlandpub.com

To Laurie Summers, my partner, and my
three favorite players, Kate, John and Caroline.
Special thanks to Glenn Altschuler and Rob Summers
for their editorial guidance and to Robert Summers
and Dorothy Summers for their ongoing support.

Table of Contents

Tables and Figures

Tables

Figures

Figures *(cont.)*

Introduction

Everyone is always kicking, young and old. Even an unborn baby is kicking.
—Sepp Blatter, Chairman of FIFA, soccer's world
governing body, on the sport's popularity.

Young Americans get a kick out of soccer. The Soccer Industry Council of America reports that more children ages six to eleven play soccer (7.9 million) than any other sport except basketball.* American colleges and universities now offer more varsity soccer programs than football programs.

What America has discovered in the last fifty years the rest of the world has known for centuries. Around the globe, soccer is by far the most popular sport. In strongholds like Europe, Central America, and South America, no other game comes close.

Many attributes give soccer its unmatched appeal. Nearly anyone can play, regardless of age, size or gender. Soccer is easy to understand, relatively safe and less expensive than most other sports. It can be played just about anywhere—on grass, sand, wood, even pavement. The fundamental skills—controlling the ball, dribbling, passing, shooting—can be learned and developed by most young players.

Players also enjoy soccer because of the way it challenges them to think. This fast-moving game does not tolerate ponderous strategies or an

1998 National Soccer Participation Survey.

1

abundance of set plays. Unlike the more strategic and deliberate games of baseball, basketball and football, soccer is a free-flowing battle stopped only by a goal, the clock or the occasional whistle. Players must make many quick decisions during the course of a match, a challenge that draws creative people to the sport.

In fact, even a player with modest talent can contribute by mastering the basics of intelligent soccer. Savvy players learn to play the ball quickly, moving into open space and support teammates, seeing the whole field, communicating well, and getting in shape to run hard for forty-five minutes without a sustained break.

As much as in any other sport, soccer players must rely on teammates to succeed. Teams made up of players who pass well and hustle to support one another usually come out on top. Raw individual skill is important but it must be used within the framework of the team to be truly effective.

At the same time, soccer presents many opportunities for players to display extraordinary individual skills. While no single player is expected to carry the team, each player has chances to stand out and to shape the defining moments of a match. This is true at every position on the field. The goalkeeper can make a diving save to ensure victory, the defender can execute a game-saving tackle, and the forward can set up or score the winning goal.

Soccer's team orientation takes the pressure off individual players in ways not seen in other popular American sports. In baseball, basketball and football, individual confrontations often determine who wins and who loses. In baseball, for example, the player who strikes out to end the game with the tying run on base may shoulder the blame for the loss. In soccer, most often teams win and lose as one; rarely do individual players carry the burden of defeat. That being so, many tentative young athletes find a comfort on the soccer field they may not find in other sports.

For all of its current popularity, soccer is a relatively young sport in America. Not until the late 1960s did communities begin to offer organized play for boys and girls. As a result, among the thousands of parents who coach youth soccer today, relatively few have played the sport themselves. An even smaller number has received the benefit of experienced coaching. Therefore, many young players are learning soccer from coaches with little or no experience.

That's where *The Soccer Starter* comes in. This book is designed for the thousands of parents and volunteers who are coaching or helping to coach youth teams but who themselves have limited background in the sport. Its mission is to provide a concise, thorough and entertaining summary that gives each coach the guidance needed to be effective in practice and during matches. Whether the players are age seven, nine or eleven, this book offers the knowledge and tools needed for coaches to succeed.

The ultimate goal is to help young players have fun, learn the game, commit to fair play, and become the best soccer players they can be.

Chapter 1

Soccer: One Sport Fits All

Soccer is the most international of all team sports. Go just about anywhere in the world, and one will find people playing soccer. On the sandlots of Brazil and in the streets of Italy, on the beaches of Japan and in the parks of England, people of all ages love to play the world's most popular sport. In fact, FIFA, the world's governing body for soccer, has more member countries than the United Nations.

Why So Many Play

Soccer appeals to so many people for many reasons. There are few physical barriers to the sport. Any person can play, regardless of age, size or gender. And while soccer is a game that was once played by males only, that is no longer the case. Around the world, and in the United States in particular, soccer has become enormously popular with women. In fact, the United States women's national team won the world championships in 1996 and 1999, often playing before sellout crowds across America and worldwide television audiences running into the millions.

Mia Hamm, the all-time leading scorer in international play for the United States, is as well known in the U.S. and around the world as any American female athlete. In fact, she is probably the most celebrated American soccer player ever.

Soccer's popularity can be traced in part to the way it challenges players to make the most of their athletic ability. The sport rewards players who develop speed, quickness, agility, strength, endurance and the capacity for team play (attributes, by the way, that serve athletes well in all sports). An accomplished soccer player has the physical talent to do well in almost any sport.

Playing soccer is also a terrific way to stay in shape. As much as any other sport, soccer demands stamina. Except for a short break at halftime and an occasional brief stoppage of play, players are on the go for the entire game. Midfielders in particular must do a lot of running because the whole field is their domain. It is not unusual for an energetic midfielder to run six or seven miles over a 90-minute game.

Soccer encourages creative thinking. There are few set plays. Players have a chance to be creative nearly every time they possess the ball. Most players possess the ball 30–40 times a game. Each time, they are challenged to make a decision. Should I dribble, pass or try to score?

Over a 90-minute game, each player has the ball for only a minute or two. When players do not have the ball, they are challenged to think about how they can move to best support their teammates. So whether a player has the ball or not, the player's creative juices are flowing.

Soccer is a great team sport, requiring that players work together to win. Seasoned players understand that each player on the team must join in a coordinated effort to maximize team performance. Above all else, team players pass the ball effectively among themselves. They know that a strong passing game is the essence of winning soccer. They also stay in excellent shape so they can run hard and support their teammates, both on attack and on defense, every moment they are on the field.

Table 1-1. Why So Many Play

- ⚽ No physical barriers
- ⚽ Develops all athletic attributes
- ⚽ Great way to get in shape
- ⚽ Encourages creative thinking
- ⚽ Rewards teamwork

The Benefits of Coaching

There are many benefits to coaching soccer.

First, it is an easy game for the prospective coach to learn, especially for those called upon to coach young players. One does not need to have played soccer to coach the sport well. What a prospective coach does need is an open mind and information. There are many misconceptions about soccer in this country—"Kick the ball with your toe"; "There is no contact in soccer"; "Soccer is a sport for people too small to play other sports." A prospective coach should put these aside. One need not be burdened with preconceptions that hinders one's ability to learn the game or coach it effectively.

Coaches must learn the rudiments of the sport. Readers can supplement what is learned from this book by talking with and observing experienced coaches and players. Readers can further add to their knowledge by watching games on television or in person. Before long, a prospective coach will grasp the fundamentals of sound soccer and be ready to coach a team to a successful season.

Coaching is a great way to serve the community. Many are so busy with work and family that they find they are not able to volunteer for community activities as much as they would like. Coaching is an ideal way to make a contribution to community life.

Coaching young players typically requires no more than four hours a week—two for one evening of practice and two for a game on the weekend.

Coaches can have a salutary impact on the lives of a dozen or so young people. They help children learn a sport that is enjoyed by nearly everyone who tries it. The game puts smiles on the faces of players, and on coaches. Through encouragement and praise, a coach can help each player build self-esteem and confidence, both on and off the field. All this is often inspiring as well as satisfying.

Coaches get an opportunity to know families in their communities. They will meet up to a dozen new families each time they coach a new team. And when their own child is on the team, he or she has the chance to make several new friends.

The greatest benefit of all is simply that coaching is tremendous fun! Coaches get to be kids again, and they draw great satisfaction from teaching young people an activity that they may well enjoy for the balance of their active lives.

Table 1-2. The Benefits of Coaching

- ⚽ Easy to learn
- ⚽ Great way to serve community
- ⚽ Positive impact on young people
- ⚽ Path to friendships

How Soccer Is Played

Soccer is an easy game to learn and play. Matches are played on rectangular fields with opposing goals centered at each end of the field. Each team has up to 11 players who work together to defend their goal and to launch attacks on the opposing goal. The field players (everyone but the goalkeeper) use their feet, thighs, chest and head to control and move the ball. Only the keeper can use his hands, and he may do so only within the penalty box in front of his goal. The team that scores the most goals wins.

How does one team manage to outscore the other? The team that has the better combination of teamwork, skill, endurance and hustle usually wins. Winning teams are more adept at controlling loose balls, at passing the ball up the field and at scoring goals.

Match the Game to the Player

Matching the game to the player is one of the most important aspects of coaching. The size of the field, the goals, the ball, the number of players and the length of games should vary depending on the age of the players. **It is critical to match these variables to the age group.** In particular, young players should not be playing by rules and conditions designed for older players.

Younger teams require fewer players and smaller fields. This gives each player the chance to touch the ball often, develop quick feet, make decisions, learn and have fun. When too many players are on the field, the less aggressive ones may feel left out and become discouraged. In addition, a field that is too large invites players to blast the ball aimlessly rather than to move the ball pass by pass up the field, as soccer is meant to be played.

Some communities may require that games be played on full-size fields, regardless of the age of the players. If so, coaches should ask the administrators to consider smaller fields for younger players. In practices,

Table 1-3. Matching the Game to Players

Age	Players	Ball Size	Field Size (l × w in yards)	Goal Size (w × h in feet)	Duration (min × periods)
5–7	4 + goalie	No. 3	40 × 30	8 × 4	10 × 4
8–9	6 + goalie	No. 4	75 × 40	12 × 6	12 × 4
10–12	8 + goalie	No. 4	90 × 50	16 × 8	30 × 2
13–15	10 + goalie	No. 5	100 × 70	24 × 8	40 × 2

the playing area should be small enough so that players are constantly around the ball.

There are no official rules that govern the variables listed above. The table on page 8, however, can serve as a guide so players of all ages can enjoy learning and playing the game.

The Laws of Soccer

Soccer was invented in England in the 11th century. Entire villages would play against each other. They would use a pig's bladder or the skull of a dead animal as the ball. There were no goals. They would play across hills and streams until one team got the ball into the center of the other team's village. Sometimes, games would last the whole day. If neither team had won by nightfall, the team closest to the other team's village would be named the winner.

Over the years, people moved from England to other parts of the world, exporting soccer with them. That's how soccer became the world's most popular sport. The sport as we know it today started to take shape in England during the 17th century.

Soccer has always been a "gentleman's" game and fair play is expected at all times. The sport is governed by 17 laws. A description of each law follows, along with some commentary designed to help coaches of young players.

Law 1: Field of Play

A regulation field is from 100 to 130 yards long by 50 to 100 yards wide. *Again, it is important to match the size of the field to the age of the participants (see Table 1-3).*

Law 2: The Ball

The ball is made of leather or some other safe, approved material. An official ball is 27 to 28 inches in circumference. *Again, coaches need to match the size of the ball to the age of the player (see Table 1-3). Encourage players to buy a leather ball and bring it to every practice and game.*

Law 3: Number of Players

A maximum of 11 players is allowed on the field for each team, one of whom must be designated goalkeeper. Teams may substitute freely during the course of a match. Any player may be replaced by a substitute

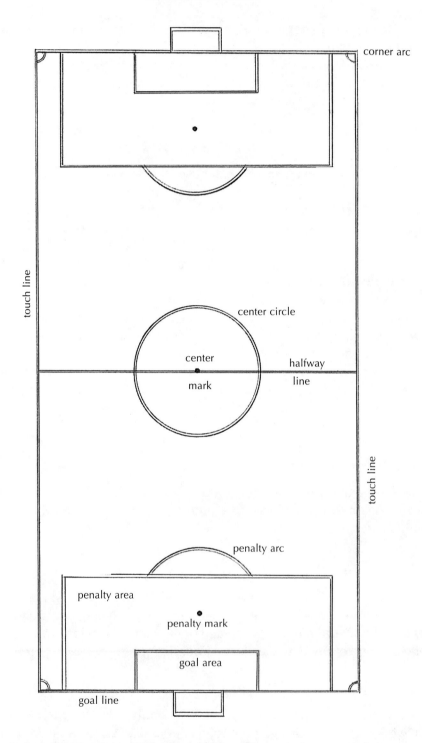

Figure 1-1. FIELD OF PLAY

during a stoppage in play, provided the referee is informed. A substitute must not come on the field until the player he is replacing has left. *Again, younger teams should play small-sided games on smaller fields (see Table 1-3).*

Law 4: Players' Equipment

Players wear a jersey, shorts, stockings, shinguards and shoes. Opposing teams should wear different colors to avoid confusion. *Equipment made of cotton works best because it absorbs sweat. Jerseys should be short-sleeved*

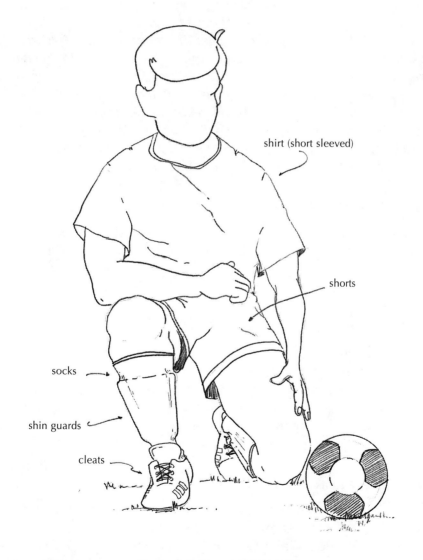

shirt (short sleeved)

shorts

socks

shin guards

cleats

Figure 1-2. PLAYER IN UNIFORM

and loose fitting. Goalkeepers should wear long sleeves to protect the arms from cuts and bruises. Goalkeepers should wear colors that distinguish them from other players and the referee. Baggy shorts are best because they allow freedom of movement. Socks should extend close to the knee to cover shinguards. Shinguards must be worn during practices and games to prevent injuries to the lower leg and protect against cuts and bruises. A player must not wear anything dangerous to another player, such as jewelry or hair clips.

Shoes are the most important piece of equipment. There are two kinds of bottoms—cleats that form part of a molded sole and cleats that screw in to the sole. Screw-in cleats must be made of leather, rubber, aluminum or plastic, and may be no longer than ¾ of an inch. Molded cleats work best on a hard field, while screw-ins provide good traction on muddy fields. For players 12 and younger, molded cleats will suffice on any field. Thereafter, serious players should own each kind. Shoes made of quality leather work best. Leather is flexible yet strong and provides good support, enabling the player to feel the ball. Shoes will last longer when maintained properly. Young players should use the laces to remove the shoes, not kick them off. Shoes should be cleaned after each use.

Law 5: Referee

One referee enforces the laws, keeps time, disciplines players, and stops the match if a player has been hurt. The referee's decision is final. *Coaches are sometimes called upon to referee games between young players (see Chapter 12).*

Law 6: Referee's Assistants

Two officials assist the referee by indicating offside; when the ball goes out of play and who gains possession via a throw-in, corner kick or goal kick; whether a penalty has been committed; and whether a goal has been scored fairly. The assistants also point out violations of the laws undetected by the referee. Referee's assistants are also called linesmen.

Law 7: Duration of Game

Regulation matches are played in two equal halves of 45 minutes, separated by a five to ten minute intermission. The referee may extend the time to make up for injuries or time wasting by a team. *Younger players should play shorter games (see Table 1-3).*

Law 8: Start of Play

The team that wins a coin toss can choose to take the kick off or defend a certain goal. At the start, both teams stand in their own halves. Players on the team without the ball must be outside the center circle at the start of the match. The ball must be played forward to start the match. A goal cannot be scored directly from the first kick. The team that did not kick off to start the game does so to start the second half.

Law 9: Ball In and Out of Play

The ball is out of play when it has wholly crossed the goal line or touchline (whether on the ground or in the air), or the game has been stopped by the referee. The ball is in play if it rebounds from a goalpost, crossbar or corner flag, and at all other times.

Law 10: Method of Scoring

A goal is scored when the whole ball has passed over the goal line, between the goal posts and under the crossbar while the ball is legally in play.

Law 11: Offside

A player is offside if the player is nearer to the opponent's goal line than the ball unless he is in his own half of the field, or there are at least two of his opponents as close or closer to their own goal. A player is called offside only if at the moment the ball touches or is played by a teammate the referee believes the player is interfering with play or an opponent, or seeking to gain an advantage by being in that position. A player is not declared offside by the referee merely because he is in an offside position, or if he receives the ball directly from a goal kick, corner kick or throw-in.

This is the most complicated rule in soccer. Work hard to understand it and spend the time needed to make sure that players understand it. Coaches may want to draw a diagram on a board and use it to explain the rule to players. During practice games, make sure to enforce the rule without exception. Each time the call is made, explain clearly why the player was in an offside position. With constant focus, young players will learn to stay onside and will not be caught robbing their team of a potential scoring opportunity.

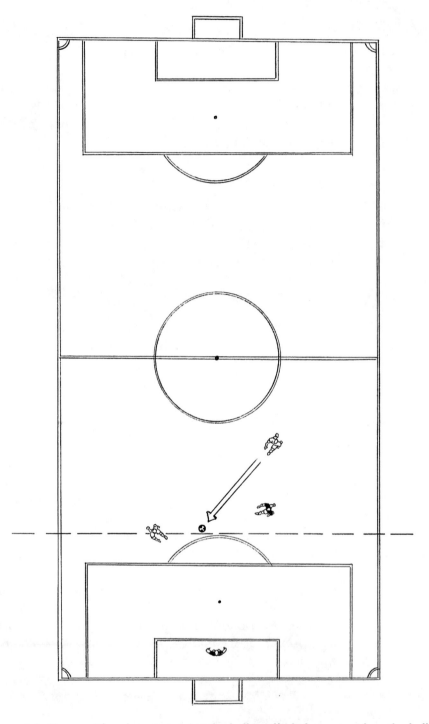

Figure 1-3. OFFSIDE: The player receiving the ball is offside because when the ball is played to him, there is only one defender (the keeper) between him and the goal.

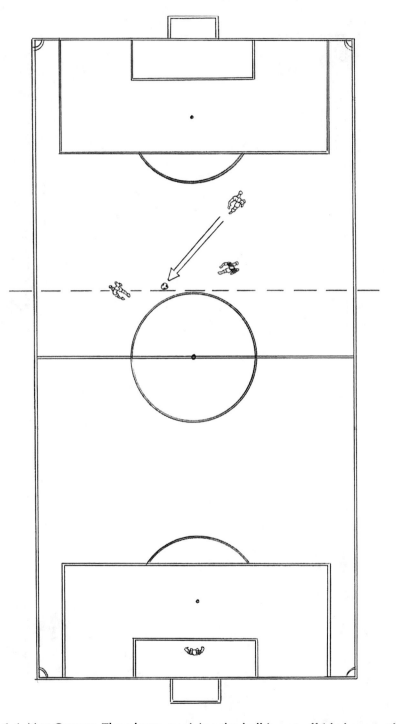

Figure 1-4. NOT OFFSIDE: The player receiving the ball is not offside because he is in his own half of the field when the ball is played.

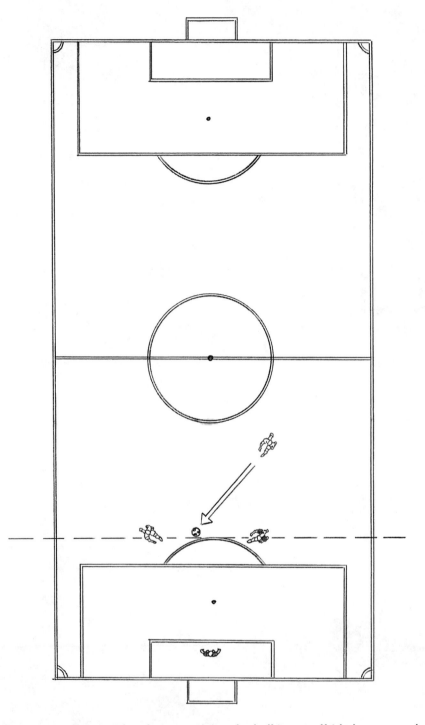

Figure 1-5. NOT OFFSIDE: The player receiving the ball is not offside because, when the ball is played, there are two opponents closer to (or as close to) the goal.

Law 12: Fouls and Misconduct

A team whose player intentionally attempts or actually kicks, trips, jumps at, charges violently, charges from behind, strikes, spits at, holds or pushes an opponent, or handles the ball is penalized by a direct free kick (see Law 13). Any one of these offenses committed in the penalty area by a defender results in a penalty kick to the attacking team (see Law 14). A team whose player commits less flagrant fouls such as offside, dangerous play, or obstruction, is penalized by an indirect free kick (see Law 13). The referee may caution a player for persistent misconduct by showing a yellow card. The referee may also send off a player for violent conduct, abusive language or persistent misconduct after receiving a caution. This is done through the showing of a second yellow card, or a red card. The player sent off may not be replaced. *Cards are not used with the youngest players. Coaches are expected to provide discipline as needed. Any player who repeatedly breaks the rules should be removed from the game and told to play by the rules.*

Law 13: Free Kick

A direct free kick is a kick from which a goal may be scored directly. An indirect free kick is a kick from which a goal cannot be scored unless

Figure 1-6. FREE KICK: A free kick is awarded after one team commits a foul.

the ball has been touched by another player before entering the goal. In both cases, the offending team's players must be at least ten yards from the ball until the ball has been touched, and the ball must be still.

Law 14: Penalty Kick

This is a direct free kick taken from the penalty spot, 12 yards from the goal. All players except the player taking the kick and the opposing goalkeeper must remain outside the penalty area and penalty arc until

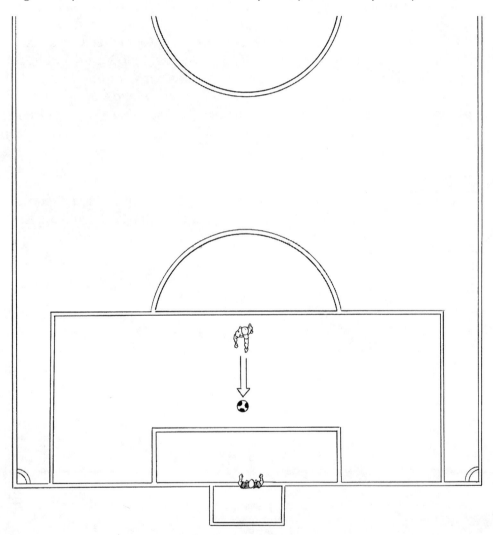

Figure 1-7. PENALTY KICK: A penalty kick is awarded after the defending team commits a foul inside the penalty area.

the ball is kicked. The goalkeeper must stay on his goal line, between the goal posts, until the ball is kicked. *The penalty spot may be closer in youth competition.*

Law 15: Throw-in

This is the method for putting the ball into play after it has crossed the entire sideline. A player from the team that did not touch the ball last takes the throw-in from the point on the sideline where the ball left the field. The player throws by using both hands to deliver the ball from behind and over the head; a part of each foot must be either on the sideline or on the ground outside of the sideline.

Through age nine, players who commit a foul on a throw-in should be instructed on what they did wrong and be given a second chance. At this age, nine times out of ten the infraction will result because the thrower lifted one foot off the ground while making the throw.

Figure 1-8. THROW-IN: When the ball crosses the side line, the team that did not touch it last puts it back into play.

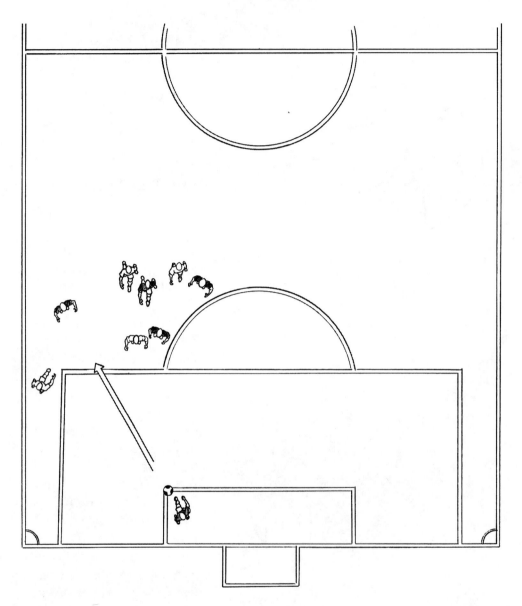

Figure 1-9. GOAL KICK: When the ball crosses the line at the end of the field last touched by the attacking team, the defending team puts it in play.

Law 16: Goal Kick

This is the method for putting the ball back into play after it has wholly crossed the goal line after being last touched by a player from the attacking team. A player from the team that was defending kicks the ball from his own goal area beyond the penalty area.

Law 17: Corner Kick

This is the method for putting the ball back into play after last being touched by a player from the defending team. A player from the attacking team kicks the ball from the corner arc nearest to where the ball left the field.

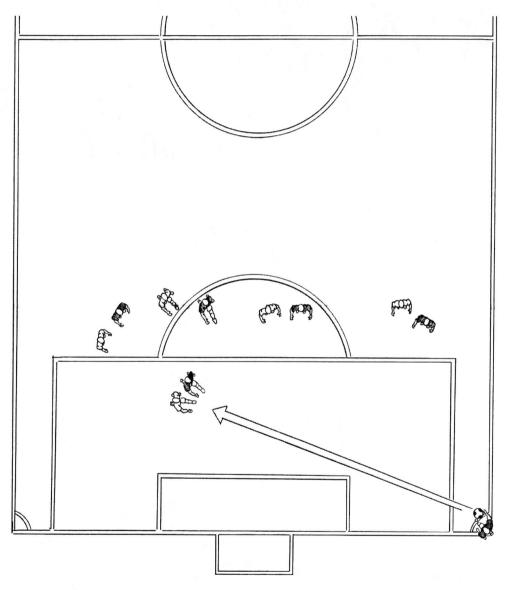

Figure 1-10. CORNER KICK: When the ball crosses the line at the end of the field last touched by the defending team, the attacking team is awarded a corner kick.

Chapter 2

Learning How to Play the Ball

A soccer player may play the ball with any part of the body except the hands and arms. Players may use their feet, thighs, chest and head to control and move the ball. The goalkeeper can use the hands and arms (see Chapter 6). Here's a closer look at how each part of the body can be used.

The Foot

The feet are a soccer player's best weapon. Through constant practice, players will learn how to control, shield, turn, dribble, pass and shoot the ball effectively. Developing these basic skills should be a priority for all young players. As players mature, coaches can encourage them to learn to move their feet in ways that deceive their opponent (see Chapter 3). Seven parts of the foot are used in soccer.

Instep

This is the hardest part of the foot, along the inside edge of the shoelaces. Players use the instep to drive the ball low and hard.

Outside

This is the area from the outer ankle to the small toe. It's used to dribble, to run with the ball, and to pass.

Inside

This is the area from the inner ankle to the big toe. The largest part of the foot, this area is used to control the ball, dribble and make short passes.

Heel

The heel can be used to pass a ball backward to a teammate.

Sole

The sole, or the bottom of the foot, is used to control a ball rolling toward a player. Skilled players also use the sole to drag the ball backward and head in the opposite direction.

Toe

Players use the toe to knock the ball out of a crowd or poke the ball off the foot of the opponent. The toe can also be used to drive the ball great distances. However, when the toe is used to kick the ball, it is difficult to control the accuracy of the kick. That's why the instep is the better choice. Encourage players to avoid using the toe to pass or shoot the ball.

Top

The top of the foot can be used to control a high ball coming toward a player. As the ball approaches, the player lifts the foot about 12 inches off the ground. When the ball is about to land on the foot, the player pulls the foot back toward the ground and "catches" the ball on top.

This is among the more difficult skills to master because the top of the foot is hard and relatively narrow. The ball must be "caught" between the toes and the instep. A ball that lands right on the toes or the instep will carom away from the player.

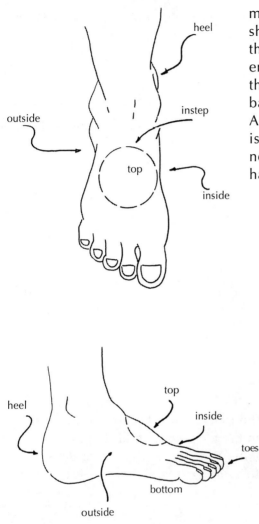

Advanced young players may want to experiment but should not be expected to use this skill. Instead, young players should favor the inside of the foot or the thigh to control balls coming at them in the air. At any age, the top of the foot is best used when no opponents are nearby so players have some margin for error.

First Kicks

It is critical that players learn the proper technique for kicking the ball. The non-kicking foot is planted next to the ball with the toes pointing toward the target. The non-kicking leg is slightly bent, and the player's arms are out for balance. The kicking leg swings back, bent at the knee. The player then straightens the leg as it is brought back down into the ball. The player keeps his head down, back straight and knee over the ball. He follows through in the direction he wants the ball to go.

Figure 2-1. *Top:* SEVEN PARTS OF THE FOOT: Soccer players use seven parts of the foot—instep, inside, outside, heel, sole, toes and top. Figure 2-2. *Bottom:* A different view.

Most young players are comfortable playing the ball with the inside and outside of the foot, but less so with the instep. A common flaw in using the instep is to keep the foot almost parallel to the ground when striking the ball. This results in the ball being played off the top of the foot—at the low end of the laces—rather than on the instep.

When demonstrating the instep kick, stress the need to point the kicking foot toward the ground before the ball is struck. By pointing the foot down the instep—the hard bone of the top of the foot—is exposed to the ball. The instep generates unmatched power, sending the ball hard and low. By contrast, a ball struck with the top of the foot will have backspin on it and will not travel far in the air or on the ground.

Figure 2-3. THE INSIDE: Players use the inside of the foot to dribble and make short passes.

Figures 2-4 (above), 2-5 (p. 27) and 2-6 (p. 28). THE INSTEP: Players use the instep to drive the ball hard and low over great distances.

Figure 2-5.

Figure 2-6.

Demonstrate this technique for the players. As appropriate, ask an experienced player to help. Work with each player to make sure they understand and use the proper form. Poor habits are hard to unlearn.

On the Ground, in the Air

Ask the players to imagine a line cutting the ball in half from side to side. To make the ball go straight and low, players kick the ball on this

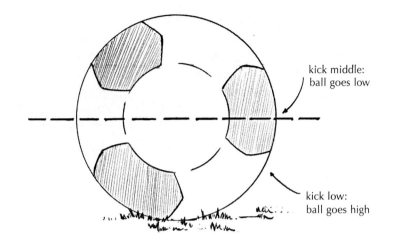

kick middle:
ball goes low

kick low:
ball goes high

Figure 2-7. THE BALL: Imagine a line through the center of the ball. Kicking at the line will keep the ball on the ground. Kicking below the line will send the ball into the air.

line. To put the ball in the air, players kick below the line. The lower the ball is struck, the higher it will go.

Players also may use their head, thighs and chest to control and move the ball.

Head

The head is another important weapon in a soccer player's arsenal. Experienced players learn to use their head to pass, shoot and clear the ball from danger.

Coaches of players ages 5 to 6 need not focus on this facet of the game. Players at this age tend to keep the ball on the ground. More so, young players are understandably not keen to throw their head in the way of a moving ball.

As players reach age 7, they begin to kick the ball in the air. Some are eager to start heading at this stage. Those who are should be encouraged to do so, while those who are not should be allowed to focus on using other parts of the body to play the ball.

By age 9, most players begin to feel comfortable heading the ball. It is at this age that heading skills can be incorporated into practices (see Chapter 11 for heading drills).

How to Head the Ball

The forehead is the best part of the head to play the ball. The forehead is flat and wide, providing a good base to generate power and accuracy. Young players simply nod their head into the ball, keeping their arms out for balance. The eyes remain open. The nod is made in the direction the player wants the ball to go.

To demonstrate, a coach should have a player lob the ball toward the coach's head from a few feet away. Gently nod the ball back. Emphasize the use of the forehead. When the ball lands any higher on the head, it will go straight up in the air or even backward. A ball played below the forehead will hurt!

As players gain more experience, they will learn to arch their backs and snap their heads at the ball, following through in the direction they want the ball to go. This extra effort puts more power into the ball. Do not expect this from young players; only the most advanced players under age 12 will use their bodies to enhance their heading skills. Heading is an advanced skill that should not be rushed onto young players.

As players mature toward their teen years, they will begin to appreciate the differences in defensive heading and offensive heading.

Heading to Defend

There are times when players are faced with a high ball coming toward the goal they are defending. Their job is to head the ball safely away from the goal. Players should practice jumping to the ball and leaning slightly back. As the ball nears, a player pushes the head and body forward and strikes the ball with the middle of the forehead. To send the ball long distances through the air, players head the ball just below the middle of the ball.

Heading to Score

Attacking players will have opportunities to score with the head, especially as they reach ages 11 and 12. The key is to nod the ball in the direction of the goal. When possible, the player should head the ball down toward the goal line. Balls coming down toward the goal are most difficult for a goalkeeper to react to. This shot is accomplished by heading the top half of the ball.

Figure 2-8. HEADING THE BALL: The keys to successful heading are knees bent, eyes open, forehead into the ball.

Figure 2-9. Using the Thigh: The thigh is used to control a ball coming in from the air.

Thigh

The best way to control a ball coming toward the mid-section is with the thigh. As the ball nears, the player lifts one leg up—with the knee bent—so that the stomach and thigh form a right angle. As the ball lands on the raised thigh, the player relaxes the leg and the ball drops at the player's feet. Arms are out for balance.

Chest

Balls coming in between the shoulders and midsection can be controlled with the chest. As the ball nears, a player pushes out the chest and lands the ball on the top part of the chest. As the ball makes contact, the player sags back and down. The player leans forward and bends at the waist. The ball caroms off the chest and back toward the feet.

As players gain more experience, they can take this skill to another level. First, encourage advanced players to chest the ball down in the opposite direction from any nearby opponent. Second, challenge them to learn how to use their chests to control a bouncing ball (see Chapter 11 for drills).

Figure 2-10. USING THE CHEST: *Left:* The chest is used to control the ball coming in at that level. As the ball nears, the player pushes out the chest. Figure 2-11. *Right:* As the ball lands, the player sags back to cushion the ball on the chest. The ball drops to the player's feet.

Chapter 3

Basic Skills
with the Ball

All soccer players should learn the basic ball skills—how to control, dribble, shield, turn, pass and shoot. Each skill is reviewed here (see Chapter 11 for drills).

Controlling the Ball

Controlling, or receiving, is the act of taking in a moving ball. This is also called collecting or cushioning the ball. The foot is used to control a ball coming on the ground. A player receiving a ball in the air can use the thigh or chest to gain control (see Chapter 2 for a review of these techniques).

Inside of the Foot

The inside of the foot works best to control a ball coming on the ground. This is the widest part of the foot, and it provides the largest surface to stop the ball. As the ball approaches, the receiver points the receiving foot sideways, opening the inside of the foot to the ball. The foot is relaxed just as the ball arrives. When a player is receiving a fast-moving ball on the ground, the player gently pulls the foot back as the ball strikes it. The foot will act as a cushion, slowing the ball and keeping it from bounding away.

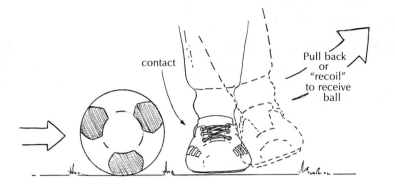

contact

Pull back
or
"recoil"
to receive
ball

Figure 3-1. CONTROLLING THE BALL WITH THE INSIDE OF THE FOOT: **The inside of the foot is used to receive a ball coming on the ground.**

Here's a useful tip that can benefit players of all ages. When controlling a pass, encourage players to control the ball 12 inches or so to either side, rather than settling it right on the foot. That way, the player can see the ball and is ready to play it right away. When the ball is settled right on the foot, the player has to look down and then nudge the ball ahead before it can be played. This is a waste of time that may enable a defender to close in and tackle the ball. The ball should be controlled in the direction of free space, rather than toward the nearest defender, to give the receiver a little extra time to think about what to do with it.

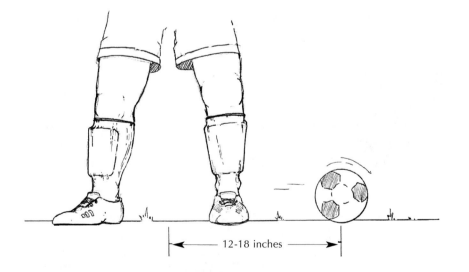

←——— 12-18 inches ———→

Figure 3-2. CONTROLLING THE BALL AWAY FROM THE BODY: **As the player receives a pass, the ball is nudged a foot or so away.**

The Sole

Players can also control a rolling ball with the bottom of the shoe. While this technique is effective, it requires that the player nudge the ball again before striking it. The inside of the foot is usually a more efficient way to gain control.

Dribbling

Dribbling, or moving with the ball, is a fundamental skill that all players should work to develop. Skilled dribblers employ clever footwork, changes of speed, fakes and superb balance to maneuver around opponents. Encourage players to experiment with all parts of their feet, in all directions. Over time, they will develop their own portfolio of moves that they will learn to execute with confidence and precision.

The two parts of the foot used most often to dribble are the inside and the outside. These are the longest parts of the foot, and they provide the most control when the ball is moved over short distances.

Players use the inside of the foot to move the ball forward or across the body. The outside of the foot is used to move the ball forward or away from the body. The arms should be out for balance and the legs loose, relaxed and slightly bent.

The ball should stay slightly ahead of the player, so the player can see it and keep a lookout for other players. As players mature, they will learn to look up from the ball between taps so they can see what is happening around them.

A good dribbler develops great "touch," or the ability to keep the ball close to his body. Skilled dribblers are also adept at changing pace and direction to avert defenders and move up the field.

Players should be encouraged to dribble with both feet. That will help them go forward, to the left and to the right with ease. The dribbling drills in Chapter 11 are designed to help assist players in building skills with both feet.

While dribbling is a vital capability, players should not overdo it. A well made pass can accomplish much more than skilled dribbling. A good pass can move a team 30 or 40 yards in a few seconds. Even the world's craftiest dribbler can't do that. The dribbler might be able to cover 40 yards with the ball, but risks losing control along the way and certainly can't do it in a few seconds.

Figure 3-3. Dribbling the Ball—Inside of the Foot: The inside of the foot is used to dribble the ball forward or across the body.

Figure 3-4. Dribbling the Ball—Outside of the foot: The outside of the foot is used to dribble the ball forward or away from the body.

Shielding

There will be many times in a match when a player seeks to control the ball while an opponent is closing in. In this situation, the player may use the body to "shield" the opponent from the ball.

There are two keys to effective shielding. First, the player with the ball keeps his body between the ball and the opponent. One side of the body faces the ball, while the other faces the opponent. Second, the player keeps the ball moving with short taps so the opponent cannot zero in and poke the ball free.

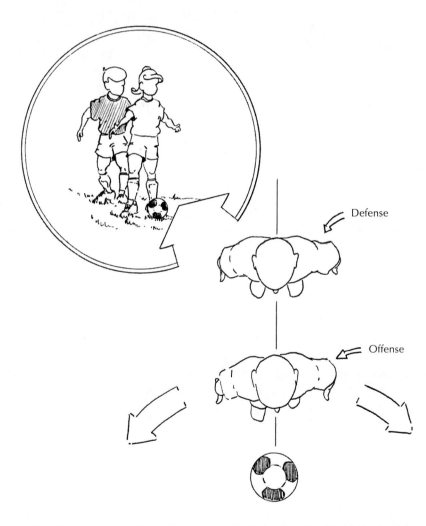

Defense

Offense

Figure 3-5. SHIELDING THE BALL: Players use their bodies to shield the ball from an opponent.

Shielding the ball allows the player in possession to maintain control and buy time. An accomplished player can ward off a defender long enough to break free into open space, get off a pass, or clear the ball from danger.

While shielding is a valuable skill, it should not be overdone. Shielding the ball for too long can stifle the momentum of the team and invite the opposition to close in. Players should keep the ball moving as soon as they get a chance.

Turning

Another key skill is turning with the ball, or changing direction. Players who are adept at turning can shake free from a tight mark and break into an open space. This gives the player time to look up, survey the field, and decide whether to continue in possession, pass or shoot.

There are four basic ways to turn with the ball.

Inside Turn

This is the simplest and most common way to change direction. The player swings a foot ahead of the ball and uses the inside to cut the ball back the other way. This works best when there is no defender nearby.

Outside Turn

This turn is more difficult to execute. As the player moves across the field, the player keeps the ball on the outside edge of his foot, away from any defenders who may be nearby. When the player senses an advantage to be gained by reversing field, the player swings the foot closest to the ball in front of the ball and then uses the outside of that foot to knock the ball back in the other direction. When executed well, this is both a safe and effective way to gain time and space on the field.

Drag Back

This is a more deceptive move that, carried out properly, can leave a defender in the dust. The player in possession places a foot on top of the ball and lets the toes slide down the other side. As soon as the ball comes to a stop, the player pulls the foot back toward the body, causing the ball to roll back in the opposite direction.

Figure 3-6.   Figure 3-7.

Figure 3-6. *Left:* TURNING—THE DRAG BACK: Players use the sole of the foot to drag the ball in the opposite direction. In step one, the foot is placed on top of the ball. Figure 3-7. *Right:* In step two, the foot is pulled back over the top of the ball, causing the ball to move back toward the player. Figure 3-8 (p. 42). In step three, the player turns and heads in the other direction with the ball.

The key to a successful "drag back" is fast execution. Any slowdown along the way will enable an alert defender to poke the ball free before the ball is brought back. Executed well, the drag back will enable the attacker to put a few yards between him and the defender.

Figure 3-8.

"Cruyff" Turn

This method of turning with the ball requires the most skill and practice but also can provide the biggest payoff. The player with the ball plants the non-kicking foot and brings the other foot down toward the ball, as if to launch a pass or shot. Rather than kick the ball, however, the player swings the foot just outside the ball and uses the outside of the big toe to tuck the ball back behind the other foot. The defender lunges to block a shot or pass that is never made, while the attacker moves away in the other direction.

Figure 3-9.

Figure 3-9. TURNING—THE CRUYFF TURN: Players can use this turn, named after the Dutchman who invented it, to fool defenders. In step one, the player brings his leg back as if to strike the ball with force. Figure 3-10 (p. 44). In step two, just before impact, the player slides the foot to the outside of the ball. Figure 3-11 (p. 45). In step three, the player uses the outside of the big toe to tap the ball behind the planted foot and then follows the ball in that direction. A well executed Cruyff turn leaves the defender lunging at a kick that is never made.

Figure 3-10.

Figure 3-11.

This move is named for the Dutchman Johann Cruyff, who mastered it in the 1970s while emerging as one of the top players in the world. It is often used when the player with the ball approaches the end line near the corner. Tightly guarded, the player fakes a crossing pass to get the defender to commit, then executes the turn to buy time and space farther from the end line.

Passing

Good passing is vital to good soccer. The best way to advance the ball toward the goal is through a series of passes among players who pass and run, pass and run. Many goals are scored after several quick passes among two or three players that move the ball over much of the field.

Constant motion and quick ball movement are the keys to an effective passing game and winning soccer. Once a player passes the ball, that player should think right away about how to support the other player who

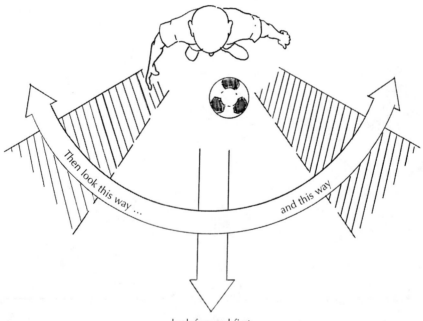

look forward first

Figure 3-12. PASSING—LEARNING TO SCAN THE FIELD: Players can improve their passing ability by staying focused on the opposing goal. First they look straight ahead for open teammates, and then they scan sideways and backward for the next best opportunity.

receives the ball. Alert players move into open space and call for the ball. They pass and move, pass and move. A team that passes well controls the ball and keeps the opponent on the defensive. The opponent expends a lot of energy chasing players and the ball.

When a player has the ball, the player should keep the head up to see opportunities developing nearby. In most cases, the best option will be to pass the ball to an open teammate who is closer to the opponent's goal. If no teammate ahead of the player is open, the player looks sideways or behind for an open teammate. Make sure players understand that it is okay to pass the ball backward to an open teammate. In many cases, this will be the best option.

Short Passes—Inside and Outside of Foot

Young players should use the inside of the foot to pass the ball along the ground to teammates nearby. This is the surest way to move the ball

Figure 3-13. PASSING—INSIDE OF THE FOOT: Players use the inside of the foot to make short passes.

Figure 3-14. PASSING–OUTSIDE OF THE FOOT: Players use the outside of the foot to make short passes.

up to 10 yards. When using the inside of the foot, the non-kicking foot is placed alongside the ball. The body is turned a little to the side to open the hips. With the toe pointed outward, the inside of the kicking foot strikes the middle of the ball. The pass is soft enough that the receiver can easily control it.

When using the outside of the foot, the kicking leg is brought straight back. As the leg moves toward the ball, the toes are pointed down. The outside of the foot strikes the ball.

Long Passes—Instep

The instep, or the top part of the foot along the shoelaces, is used to produce low, hard drives. Most long passes and shots are taken with the instep. The head stays down. Arms are raised slightly to provide balance. The kicking toe stays pointed at the ground as contact is made. Both knees are kept slightly bent. The kicking leg swings up after the ball is struck, following through in the direction of the target. The head stays down until the follow through is completed.

Figure 3-15. PASSING WITH THE INSTEP: Players use the instep to pass the ball over long distances. The kicking leg is brought back, with the eyes focused on the ball. As the leg comes into the ball, the toes are pointed down, exposing the instep of the ball. The instep strikes the ball, and the player follows through in the direction of the target.

The Wall Pass

The "wall pass" is one of the most simple and effective ways to move the team forward. When a player encounters an opponent, the player should look for an open teammate on one side or the other. He or she passes the ball to that teammate, runs around the opponent and receives the pass back from his teammate. The player has used the teammate as a wall, playing the ball off the "wall" to get around the opponent. Many of the drills in Chapter 11 are designed to encourage players to execute the wall pass.

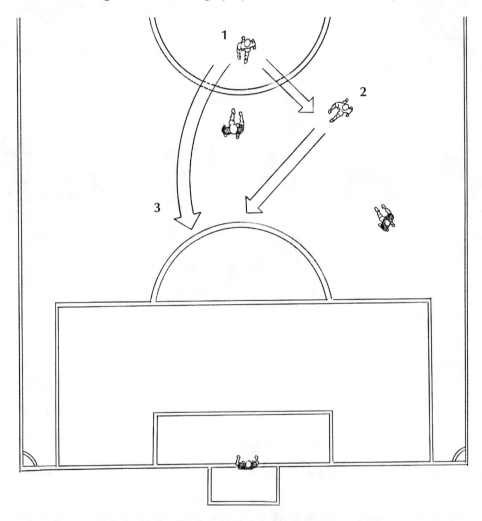

Figure 3-16. THE WALL PASS: The wall pass is an effective way to move the ball around opponents. Player 1, confronted by a defender, passes the ball to a teammate, Player 2, on the side. Player 1 runs around the opponent, and his teammate delivers the ball back to him. Player 2, in effect, serves as a wall for Player 1.

Five Keys to a Successful Pass

Pace

The passer should make it as easy as possible for the receiver to control the ball. Ideally, the receiver will have to touch the ball just once to gain full control and move ahead. Passes to unmarked teammates nearby should be soft. Longer passes need to be struck with force to get to the target without being intercepted.

Accuracy

Players passing the ball to a stationary teammate should play the ball to the teammate's foot or slightly in front of the teammate. Passes made to a moving player should be played ahead of the player so he can run comfortably onto the ball. A running player receiving a pass should not have to stop, or even slow down, to collect the ball. Remember, the ball is easiest to control when it is on the ground. This goes for throw-ins, too. The ball should be tossed to the teammate's feet, where it can be controlled and moved right away.

Timing of the Pass

The passer should try to "connect" with the intended receiver—through eye contact or intuitive feel—before making the pass. The passer should be sure that the receiver expects the pass to be made and then pass the ball as soon as the teammate is ready to receive it.

Timing of the Run

The receiving player needs to make sure that the player with the ball has clear possession and has a clear passing lane before calling for the ball or making a run.

Timing is critical. Lots of passes are never made, or end up as stray balls, because the passer and receiver failed to "connect."

The Passer's Reaction

As soon as the pass is made, the passer should be moving into open space to support other teammates. Too many players stand and watch a pass, like an artist admiring a painting. There's no time for that in soccer!

Table 3-1. Five Keys to a Good Pass
☺ Pace
☺ Accuracy
☺ Timing of Pass
☺ Timing of Run
☺ The Passer's Reaction

Encourage Players to Think Beyond the Obvious Pass

Once a player develops full leg strength, encourage the player to be creative and think beyond the obvious pass. Of course, this is where we are reminded that soccer is a team sport! An inventive passer needs creative, energetic teammates who make good runs into open space. This is the beauty of soccer—two or more imaginative players linking up to launch a creative attack at the goal. Clever passers, especially midfielders, can have a huge impact on the flow of a match.

Shooting

Great shooters are hard to find. Putting the ball past a skilled goalkeeper is a difficult task. But through hard work and practice, players of all ages can learn to consistently create and execute scoring opportunities.

Stress the following technical points: a player should keep the knee over the ball and the back straight. The player should keep the head down and eyes on the ball until contact is made. The player follows through with the kicking foot to maximize power. Demonstrate the proper technique, over and over, calling in experienced players to help as necessary.

Table 3-2. Shooting Basics
☺ Head down
☺ Knee over the ball
☺ Back straight
☺ Follow through

Many opportunities to score come from about 15 to 25 yards from the goal. From this distance, young players should favor the instep, the hard part of the foot under the shoelaces. On tap-ins, players should use the inside of the foot. Once players reach their teens, they will be prepared to experiment with shooting with the outside of the foot.

Ground Rules for Shooting

Here are some ground rules for players to follow when shooting the ball.

Shoot Fast

Any player close enough to shoot is likely to have at least one defender closing in. Tell players to shoot as soon as they think they have the best chance to score a goal.

Shoot Hard

Hard balls are more difficult to handle. Encourage players to shoot with the instep, following the technique outlined above. Form is more important than leg speed. Swinging too hard will likely send the ball high or wide or both.

Shoot Low and Toward the Corners

When the ball comes toward a keeper in the air, the keeper's hands can be used to catch or deflect the shot. For low balls, the keeper must dive.

Shoot to the Far Post

If the shot is headed wide, a teammate may be able to run onto it and direct it into the net. There is no such opportunity on shots struck wide of the near post.

Sneak a Peek

As players mature toward their teenage years, encourage them to steal a glance at goal before they shoot. The shooter might see that the goalie is leaving more space on one side than the other. The shooter might sense that the keeper is too far off the line, giving the shooter an opportunity to loft the ball over the keeper and under the crossbar. Sometimes, one quick peek can give the shooter the edge needed to put the ball away.

Okay Coach, So When Do I Shoot?

There is no easy answer to this question. As Rick Davis, former captain of the United States National Team, said: "I haven't learned how to teach players to score goals. You can teach people to defend, to shoot, but you can't teach them how to score."

Some players pass up good chances to score to try to get closer to the goal. But they often lose the ball before they have another chance to shoot.

A good rule to follow: if a player thinks there is a real chance to score, and there are no better options available, the player should take a crack at it. At the same time, if the player is about to shoot but then sees a teammate in a better position to score, the player should make the pass.

As players spend more time in shooting situations, they will instinctively sense what to do. That's another reason why short-sided games are so valuable—each player is constantly involved in scoring opportunities and is forced to make decisions with the ball.

A final point on shooting: young players often shy away from shooting for fear that they will miss. Encourage players to take reasonable shots. When the shot is saved or goes wide, reinforce the effort with simple praise.

Trickery

Young players can learn to move their bodies in ways that throw their opponents off balance. They lean with their hips one way and then dart off in the other direction. They move their feet quickly to lead an opponent one way before moving in another direction. They fake a long kick, only to nudge the ball around a vulnerable defender.

Players through age nine are best to concentrate on developing their basic dribbling skills and experimenting with the deceptive moves described above. As players reach ten and older, they can add to their bag of tricks by practicing more refined feints. Here are some of the more advanced ways players can use their feet to fool a defender.

Step-over

The player with the ball is dribbling toward a defender. The player moves one foot across the body toward the ball. The foot continues just over the ball and is planted on the other side. As soon as the foot lands, the player uses the outside of the foot to nudge the ball in the other direction.

Figure 3-17 (above). TRICKERY—THE STEP-OVER: The player moves one foot across the body and toward the ball. Figure 3-18 (p. 56). Just before the foot touches the ball, the foot is raised over the ball and planted on the other side. Figure 3-19 (p. 57). As soon as the foot plants, the player uses the outside of the foot to nudge the ball in the other direction.

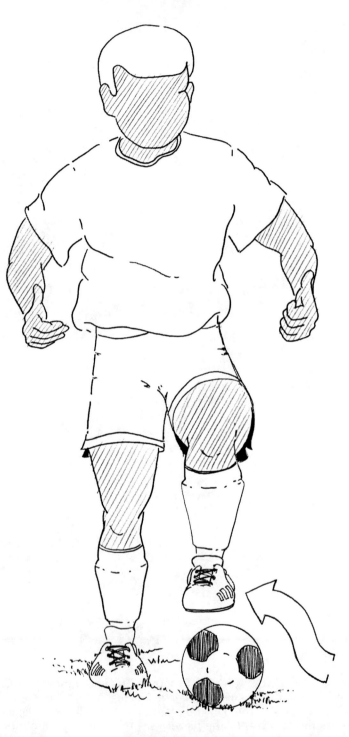

Figure 3-18.

Figure 3-19.

Fake Shot

Another effective move is to fake a shot. A player winds up as if to strike the ball. The defender freezes, preparing to block the shot. But the attacker slows his or her leg on the downswing and merely taps the ball past the defender for a better shot. With practice, many players can develop this fake and use it well in competition.

Fake Pass

Another common trick is to fake a pass to a teammate. The opponent moves to block the "pass," thereby enabling the player to quickly run past with the ball.

Wrong-foot

Crafty dribblers use another move to get the opponent moving in the wrong direction. With the ball in front of them, they raise one foot up and move it away from the body and toward the ball. This motion, accented by hips moving in the same direction, suggests to the defender that the player plans to take the ball in that direction.

Instead, the dribbler's foot goes just beyond the ball and plants outside the ball. As soon as that first foot hits the ground, the player uses the outside of the other foot to push the ball in the opposite direction.

Tap Back

A player winds up as if to kick the ball in one direction. At the last second, the player lifts the foot over the ball and uses the inside of the big toe to tap the ball behind the other leg. The defender is left trying to block what seems to be a pass, while the player with the ball is heading in the other direction (also known as the Cruyff Turn).

Here's an important point to convey to players: The player with the ball should not make a planned move until sufficiently close to the defender. If a player makes the move from too far away, the defender will have time to recover and tackle the ball. With practice, players will develop the ability to maneuver at the right time.

There are no limits to the ways in which a player can deceive an opponent. Encourage players to be creative and to try different fakes in practice and in the backyard to gain confidence. Over time, they will learn to execute them with enough precision to use them consistently on the field.

Use Both Feet!

From the beginning, encourage players to develop skills with both feet. Young players will favor their strong foot, and well they should, because one strong foot is much better than two average ones. In fact,

Figure 3-20 (above). TRICKERY—THE WRONG FOOT: The player moves the outside of the foot toward the ball. Just before contact, the player raises the foot over the ball and plants it on the other side. Figure 3-21 (p. 60). As soon as the first foot lands, the player swings the outside of the other foot into the ball, taking it in the opposite direction of the original fake.

Figure 3-21.

some of the best players in the history of the sport used only one foot (Argentina's Maradona, Germany's Beckenbauer).

That said, players skilled with both feet have an advantage in just about every facet of the game. They can control the ball easily, no matter from what angle they receive the ball. They can dribble and turn effectively, using the inside and outside of both feet to maneuver in tight spaces. They can pass and shoot with confidence, whether the ball sits at the left foot or right foot.

Instill in players that a strong second foot will make them better players. Encourage them to use both feet in drills. Every now and then in practice, have players focus on their weaker foot. A "left foot only" drill or game is one way to make this work. Coaches can even require players to use only their weaker foot for an entire practice. When the team takes a huge lead in a game, tell players to play only with their weaker foot. No player wants to be known as the one who uses the left foot "only to get on the bus"!

Chapter 4

Basic Skills
Without the Ball

In a typical game, a team may have the ball for one-third of the time, the other team may have it for one-third, and it may be free for the other third. That means each team is trying to win the ball for two-thirds of the match!

When players begin playing competitive soccer, the field should be small enough that each player can go after the ball from one end of the field to the other. When their team has the ball, encourage players to attack the opposing goal with vigor. When their team loses possession, players should pursue the ball with the same energy and intensity displayed when they have the ball. Divide praise evenly among the goal scorers and the ball retrievers.

With players through age 7, coaches are best to provide only a general introduction to the concept of defense. At this age, there is no player-to-player guarding. Players will want to chase the ball all over the field. Unrefined hustle is what to expect at that age. The players are too young to grasp the more advanced concepts of defending.

After a year or two of experience, however, players will begin to experiment with ways to tackle the ball from an opponent. With the proper training, young players can learn to pursue the ball, pressure the opposing team and win the ball. Coaches can begin to focus on the skills covered in this chapter when players are about eight or nine.

Jockeying

An aggressive player learns to shadow an opponent well and thus discourage the other team from passing the ball to that opponent. There are times, though, when every defender has to guard a player with the ball.

When an opponent has the ball, the defender can "jockey" or shadow the player. This is done by staying about a yard in front of the player with the ball, no matter where the player moves, across or down the field. A defender skilled at jockeying is comfortable moving laterally and backward. Jockeying slows the opponent down and discourages any intended runs. It also creates pressure that may cause the opponent to make a mistake. The defender staggers his legs so the attacker cannot push the ball between them.

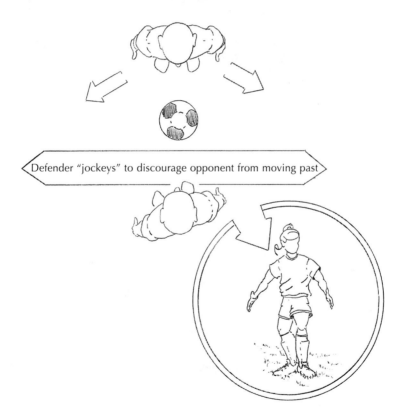

Defender "jockeys" to discourage opponent from moving past

Figure 4-1. JOCKEYING: Jockeying is a defensive tactic designed to slow down the player with the ball. The defender moves to stay a few feet in front of the player with the ball. He does not challenge for the ball; he merely discourages the attacking player from trying to get by.

Tackling

Skillful defenders learn how to "tackle" the ball, or strip it away from the opposing player. This is where soccer becomes a more physical game, because tackling often brings two players together in a clash over the ball. As long as players tackle within the rules, this is a relatively safe part of the game. There are three basic ways to tackle the ball.

Block Tackle

This is the most common way of taking the ball from an opponent. The defender plants the inside of one foot in the path of the ball, stopping

Figure 4-2. Block Tackle: The block tackle is the most common way to take the ball from an opponent.

the opponent and jarring the ball free. Sometimes the ball squirts away, sometimes the defender comes away cleanly with it. Either way, the defender has accomplished his goal of dispossessing the attacking player.

Poke Tackle

Defenders use their toes to knock the ball off the foot of the attacker. The poke tackle is used to separate the ball from the attacker, not to gain control. Defenders use this tactic when they are close enough to the ball that they think they can strike it before the opponent does.

Figure 4-3. POKE TACKLE: The defender, sensing he can touch the ball before he attacking player can, lunges with his toes to poke the ball off the foot of the attacker.

Slide Tackle

The defender slides along the ground, mimicking a feet-first slide in baseball. The defender bends one leg back, slides on the hip and kicks the ball with the other leg while sliding on the ground. The goal is to use the front foot to knock the ball away from the opponent. This tackle is often used as a last-chance effort to stop a streaking player from moving ahead for a clear shot at goal. The defender must play the ball first, not the player.

Defenders should be careful when using the slide tackle in their own penalty area. If the tackle is not timed right, the defender may take down the player before reaching the ball. That would result in a foul that leads to a penalty kick.

It is important that young players learn to tackle the ball with their feet. They should use their body only to provide balance and support.

Figure 4-4. SLIDE TACKLE: The defender executes a baseball slide, knocking the ball away with the front foot.

NO TACKLE ZONE

Figure 4-5. No Tackling from Behind: **Players should never try to tackle the ball from behind the player in possession. This is dangerous and it could lead to the ejection of the tackler.**

Players should tackle the ball, not the opponent's legs. An important point to make: **PLAYERS NEVER TACKLE FROM BEHIND**. Doing so can cause serious injury at any age. The offender may be expelled from the match and, if so, may not be replaced.

Shouldering

Players may use their shoulders as they battle for a loose ball. When a player comes shoulder to shoulder with an opponent in pursuit of a

Figure 4-6. Shouldering: Players may use their shoulders to exert pressure on an opponent, but only within the rules of play.

free ball, the player should stay firm and try to use the body to gain the inside track to the ball. Players cannot lunge into an opponent, but they can subtly exert pressure to gain advantage. As players gain experience, they will become more adept at using their bodies to forge an edge, within the rules of the game.

Chapter 5

The Field Positions

There are four basic positions in soccer—forward, midfielder, defender and goalkeeper.

Most adult teams play in one of two formations—four defenders, four midfielders and two forwards (4-4-2), or four defenders, three midfielders and three forwards (4-3-3). (When using numbers to describe a formation, start with the number of defenders and work forward).

Players younger than age 8 are merely learning the basic techniques of soccer. Coaches should not be concerned with "positions" during these first years. Instead, encourage young players to try to play the entire field—to go forward when a teammate is attacking and to retreat and defend when the other team approaches your goal. The field should be small enough that players can move from one end to the other regularly without wearing down.

As players gain more experience, they will begin to appreciate the differences between positions. They will begin to see that each player on the team is expected to make a distinct contribution, depending on the position being played. Once players have a few years of experience, coaches can introduce the defender-midfielder-forward concept, even in small-sided games.

Here's a closer look at what to expect from players in each position.

Forward

The forward's job is to score goals! They play mostly in the attacking half of the field where they lead the offense and try to set up and finish scoring opportunities. Forwards make runs to get open for passes. They may run back toward midfield, across the field or ahead into the corners. Savvy forwards mix up their runs to keep the defenders guessing where they will go next. When they receive the ball in the front third of the field, they focus on attacking the goal.

Table 5-1. Playing Forward

- ⚽ Work to get open
- ⚽ Control the ball and face the goal
- ⚽ Work with teammates to create chances
- ⚽ Shoot, shoot, shoot!

Effective forwards are able dribblers, passers and shooters. They dribble to break free from tight marks and get off shots. They pass to set up teammates for shots at the goal. And they must develop a powerful, accurate shot that makes them a threat to score from nearly anywhere in the attacking third. The best scorers also learn to shoot fast before defenders swarm in.

Forwards also must be prepared to play defense as needed. When the other team has the ball, a forward must mark the player who is marking him.

Midfielder

In many ways, midfield is the most demanding position. The best midfielders make an impact from one end of the field to the other. At the attacking end, they set up the offense for rushes on the opposing goal. In the middle, they fight to win loose balls, gain control and coordinate

---

Table 5-2. Playing Midfield

- ⚽ Cover the whole field
- ⚽ Ignite the attack
- ⚽ Support the defense
- ⚽ Run the whole game

---

the attack. On defense, they work to keep the opposition from creating scoring chances.

Midfielders need to be in peak physical condition so they can run for the entire game. A productive midfielder is constantly in motion, sparking the attack, chasing down stray balls or defending against attacks on their goal. It is not unusual for a midfielder to cover six to seven miles in a 90-minute match.

Midfielders also must be adept at controlling, dribbling and passing the ball, because they often operate in tight spaces, surrounded by the opposition. A well-rounded midfielder also possesses a potent shot that can be unleashed from up to 30 yards away.

Defender

Defenders have one priority—keep the other team from scoring. The most effective defenders keep the opponent from receiving the ball in the first place. They mark the opponent tightly, discouraging the other team from even playing the ball toward the player they are guarding.

When an opponent does get the ball, the defender must keep that player from getting past. Top defenders develop skills and instincts that help them shut down an opponent with the ball. They have quick feet, they focus on the ball not the opponent, and they develop a keen sense of when to strike (see Chapter 4 for tackling techniques).

The best defenders are also skilled with the ball and play a role in the attack. Once they gain possession, they distribute the ball to ignite the offense. The most ambitious defenders make periodic runs toward the other goal and move into position to convert a crossing pass into a shot on goal. They are often unguarded on these forays because the forwards on the opposing team are caught by surprise or winded.

How does a coach determine which players should play which position?

Table 5-3. Playing Defense

⚽ Keep the ball away from the goal
⚽ Mark the opponents tightly
⚽ Clear the ball out of danger
⚽ Pass well to start the attack

Young players should experiment at all positions. Each one requires unique abilities. Forwards must be able to control, dribble and shoot. Midfielders must control and distribute the ball well and they must be conditioned to cover the whole field. Defenders must be adept at marking the opponent and taking the ball. Goalkeepers need to be quick, agile and surehanded.

Over time, players tend to develop skills and interests that are best suited to one position. In most cases, this happens after several seasons of play. Of course, through good coaching, players with potential can be developed to play any position.

Chapter 6

The Goalkeeper

The goalkeeping position is different from the field positions and therefore may present a special challenge. Most young players want the ball at their feet, with the promise of a shot on goal never far off. For those players, the thought of standing in front of their own goal for the entire match is a less than appetizing proposition.

Furthermore, the goalkeeper ("keeper") may endure long periods with little or no action. All of sudden, that same keeper may come under attack and surrender the game-losing goal. In this worst-case scenario, no young player would want to return to the position.

Still, goalkeeper is an absolutely vital position at all but the youngest ages, and young players with an interest should be encouraged to try it. These players should experiment with field positions as well so that they experience every facet of the game. If by age 12 a player favors playing goalkeeper, that would be an appropriate time to focus exclusively on the position.

The critical difference between goalkeeper and the other positions is that the keeper can use the hands.

In many ways, the goalkeeper is the most important player on the field. The keeper is the last line of defense and often the first line of offense, launching a quick throw or kick to ignite the attack. The winning keeper often gets major credit for the victory; the losing keeper is occasionally the goat. An exceptional goalkeeper can keep an inferior team in the game, while an inconsistent keeper can spell defeat for what is, overall, a superior team.

Up through age eight, the focus should be on the fundamentals – how a keeper should be positioned, and how to catch, throw and kick (see Chapter 11 for drills).

Positioning

First, keepers should learn to stand a few feet in front of the goal line. Inexperienced players sometimes stand right on the line. When they catch a hard shot, their momentum can take them into the goal. They concede a score instead of blocking one.

Figure 6-1. BASIC POSITIONING: The keeper stands on balls of feet, hands facing outward, chest high.

When preparing to save a shot, a keeper should be on the balls of his or her feet, with the feet shoulder-length apart, and knees slightly bent. The hands are open and half-raised. From this stance, the keeper is ready to move quickly in any direction.

In addition, young players should learn to position themselves based on how the ball moves across the field. As the ball moves one way, the keeper should move with it, using the posts as guides. That way, the keeper will learn how to face an oncoming threat from the best possible angle.

Goalkeepers must be able to cover a lot of ground in a hurry. An agile keeper learns to move forward, backward, sideways, and up and down with ease. The keeper can leap to catch, deflect or punch high

Figure 6-2. JUMPING TECHNIQUE: **The keeper jumps off one leg, with the other leg bent at the knee.**

balls, and dive to block low shots. Keepers, when jumping for the ball, will go higher taking off from one foot. The knee in the opposite leg is raised into the body for extra lift.

Catching

Keepers are often challenged to catch or deflect hard shots from close range. The best can react fast with their hands and hold onto hard shots. Keepers should focus on catching the ball at the point farthest from their body. To catch a ball above the waist, the arms should be extended and the thumbs should meet as they reach for the ball (forming the letter, "W").

To catch a ball below the waist, the keeper brings the hands together, with fingers toward the ground and thumbs pointing out (forming the letter, "M"). Again, if the ball is mishandled, the body serves as a backstop.

Keepers use their eyes to catch well. They should follow the ball into their hands with their eyes. Keepers should **never take their eyes off the ball** while the ball is in play.

Experienced keepers learn to use their bodies as an extra line of protection when catching the ball. A high ball that slips through the hands

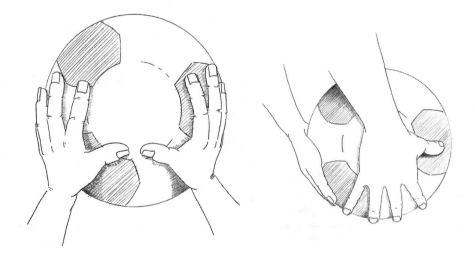

Figure 6-3. *Left:* CATCHING THE BALL ABOVE THE WAIST: When catching the ball above the waist, the keeper forms "W" with the hands. **Figure 6-4.** *Right:* CATCHING THE BALL BELOW THE WAIST: When catching the ball below the waist, the keeper forms "M" with his hands.

will be stopped by the chest. A low ball that slides through the fingers will carom off the body, which is kept behind the hands. For faster rolling balls, the keeper bends down on one knee to catch it directly in front of the body.

By bringing the hands and the arms out to meet the ball, the keeper controls a live ball at the earliest possible moment.

Throwing

When the keeper gains possession, the ball should be delivered to an open teammate who has time to dribble or pass. The faster a keeper can do this, the better the team can counterattack. This is true at any age! As soon as control is gained, a keeper should look for an open teammate on the flanks of the field. The keeper steps up quickly to the top of the goal area and rolls the ball to the open player.

The underhanded throw, or roll, is the best way for a young keeper to pass up to 20 yards. The overhand throw is the best way to deliver the

Figure 6-5. UNDERHAND ROLL: The best way for a keeper to deliver the ball to a player close by is with the underhanded roll. The ball is released low to the ground, so that it arrives on the ground, where it is easiest to control.

Figure 6-6. OVERHAND THROW: Keepers use the overhand throw to send the ball longer distances.

ball over longer distances. Young keepers find the underhanded roll the easiest way to distribute the ball. Focus on it in practice (see Chapter 11 for goalkeeper drills). Punting the ball, or dropping it and kicking it out of the air, will come later.

Under a new rule, keepers may now take as many steps as they like within the penalty box after gaining possession. The ball must be released within six seconds. For players age 10 and younger, there is no need to follow this time constraint to the letter.

As keepers mature and the quality of play improves, the advanced skills may be developed.

Diving

Diving is a technique best introduced slowly and with caution. A good way to get started is to have players start on their knees. From there,

Figure 6-7. Diving: The keeper bends at the knees, pushes off the ground and thrusts himself sideways into the path of the ball. Arms are extended in unison over the head, coming together to grasp the ball.

they can lunge to the side to learn to stop a rolling ball (see Chapter 11 for goalkeeper drills).

Once keepers are comfortable with this lunging motion, they can be taught to dive from a standing position. When teaching this, stress that the players should land on their sides. Demonstrate for the players. Once players see their coach do it without harm, they will feel more comfortable taking those first few dives. And once they make a few diving saves, they will no longer worry about getting hurt. They will worry only about keeping the ball out of the goal.

Stress that when diving, goalkeepers should attempt to get both hands on the ball. They should focus on the "W" hand position to secure the ball as they dive.

Foot Skills

A rule introduced a few years ago prohibits keepers from handling passes from teammates (unless the ball is played backward with a part of the body other than the foot). As a result, keepers are called on to use their feet much more today. They need to be comfortable controlling passes from their teammates and clearing the ball with powerful, accurate kicks. While this rule is not always enforced at younger ages, young keepers should focus on foot skills and strength just the same.

Decisiveness

Experienced keepers are challenged to think quickly on their feet. Many times in a game they will face tough decisions. Two examples are provided in this section.

When my opponent is coming at me one-on-one, should I come out to cut down the angle, or stand my ground? By coming out straight into the path of the ball, the keeper gives the shooter less space to shoot into. At the same time, the keeper runs the risk that the player will shoot the ball over the keeper's head or dribble around and score. In most cases, the keeper is better off coming out, because staying on the line provides

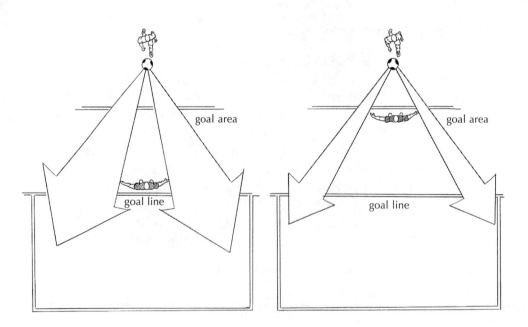

goal area

goal line

goal area

goal line

Figure 6-8. CUTTING DOWN THE ANGLE: **The keeper comes out of his goal to give the attacker less room to shoot into.**

little chance of stopping a shot, unless the ball is struck right at the keeper. Goalkeepers should come out quickly and maintain their balance so they can react to a shot at any time.

Keepers have three basic options in one-on-one situations:

1. The Challenge—The keeper can run right at the attacker. As they close in, they dive at the ball and the feet of the attacker in an attempt to win the ball. In order to protect themselves, keepers should ball their body into a semi-fetal position as they dive with their hands extended toward the ball.

2. The Counter and Delay—The keeper runs at the attacker and positions the body between the ball and the goal. The keeper can choose to stay a few yards away from the attacker and try to anticipate the attacker's next move. The keeper moves the body to counter the attacker's moves, keeping the ball between the keeper and the attacker. This tactic can sometimes force the attacker to shoot the ball into the keeper, create a delay so help can arrive, or even give the keeper a chance to win the ball with the feet or a dive.

3. The Deception—As soon as the keeper realizes this is a one versus one situation, the keeper makes a bold advance toward the attacker. After advancing only a few yards, the keeper stops and takes a regular stance, with arms out like wings. This tactic can succeed by hurrying nervous attackers into shooting wide or right at the keeper. This is especially effective against young or inexperienced attackers.

Should I leave my line and try to catch that crossing pass, or stay back and hope my teammate clears it away? An experienced keeper knows when he or she can beat the opponent to a ball floated into the box.

Keepers have three basic rules to follow in this situation:

1. Keepers should go for every ball they know they can win.

2. Keepers should consider the area right in front of the goal—the six-yard box—to be their domain. The keeper must try to control any balls played into this area.

3. The keeper's hands should be able to reach over the head of any opponent.

Concentration

Instill in keepers the need to remain focused at all times. This can be a challenge, especially with younger players on a dominant team. Sometimes the keeper can go long stretches without being involved. Under such conditions, a young mind may drift. Keep watch and provide encouragement from the sideline as needed—"Stay focused," "Head in the game."

With experience, a keeper will learn how to read the flow of the match and develop an ability to anticipate what might happen next. As the other team draws near, the keeper bounces on the balls of both feet, engaged in the rhythm of play and ready to move quickly when the ball is played.

Leadership

Goalkeepers should be field generals. The keeper has a full view of the field and sees the entire game developing. When the keeper sees something that teammates need to know, such as an opponent running unmarked, the keeper alerts teammates. When the keeper wants the ball, the keeper yells out so that teammates know to get out of the way.

Chapter 7

Six Keys to Smart Play

As much as any other sport, soccer is played with both the body and the mind. Each player has the ball for only two or three minutes during a full game. What the player does with the ball is crucial to the team's success. At the same time, what that player does when he or she doesn't have the ball is vital, too. How the player moves to support the offense and the defense has an important impact on the flow of the match.

Here are some ways players can increase their value to the team, whether they have the ball or not. Bear in mind that these concepts are not learned at one practice or even in one season. As players mature, they will gradually learn these principles and put them to effective use on the field.

Think Fast, Play Fast

The best soccer in the world is played at a fast pace. Teams gain an advantage by keeping the ball moving and beyond the reach of their opponents. When a team passes the ball effectively, the other team is kept on the chase, expending precious energy.

Smart players do not dither with the ball. They look for ways to crank up the attack, either with a crisp pass or by dribbling into the clear while teammates move to get open. They do not give the opponent time to rest, mentally or physically.

At the same time, players should not feel pressed to move the ball right away. It may be that when they gain possession, there are no immediate options available. Players should survey the field first, consider their options and then get on with it. Tell players that once they have the ball under control, keep it moving.

Move Without the Ball

Players who do not have the ball must not stand and watch the game go by. Instead, when a teammate has the ball, players should think about how they can move to support the teammate. They should look for a space in which they can receive a pass and move quickly into that space. A player who is not closely guarded and well positioned should call for the ball. Then, after a teammate passes a ball to this player, the teammate should run into space and look for a return pass. This "pass and move" system is the best way to move the ball toward the goal.

When watching a team play, coaches naturally focus on the player with the ball. As new coaches become more comfortable with the game, they should focus on other players. See which ones are running to support the teammate who has the ball. Praise the players who make these supporting runs. When a player is not moving to support a teammate, encourage that player to do so. Players who are active "off the ball" tend to touch the ball and influence a game much more than those who "ballwatch." Get ballwatchers into the match.

Learn to See the Whole Field

An experienced player learns to keep the head up while moving about the field, staying alert to the full range of options. A player can be in five situations during a game: the player has the ball, a teammate has the ball, the opponent has the ball, the ball is out of play, or the ball is free. A player who keeps the eyes open has an edge in each situation.

When a Player Has the Ball

The player should look for teammates and identify all available passing lanes. With this full view, the player can best decide whether to shield, dribble, pass or shoot.

When a Teammate Has the Ball

The player can scan the field for an open space to run into. Once into the space, the player calls for the ball. Players should not be lulled into simply watching their teammates. They should always look for ways to support other players, and so the team.

When the Other Team Has the Ball

A player should try to anticipate where the ball will go next. Through practice, a player will develop the instinct to sniff out a pass, step in and break up the play. Many goals are scored after an alert player steals a pass near the opposing goal.

When the Ball Is Out of Play

Opponents sometimes turn their backs or take a breather. By keeping an eye on the game, a player may be able to make a quick throw-in or a short corner kick to an open teammate.

When the Ball Is Free

Players who stay focused can react immediately and get a jump on the opponent. A player should approach a free ball with the head up to quickly assess options **before** getting to the ball.

Communicate Well

Players who keep their head up will also be able to communicate effectively with their teammates. A player who learns to see the whole field will spot opportunities and threats that teammates may not see. When that happens, the player can alert teammates to any situation.

For example, a player may be able to tell a teammate that a defender is closing in from behind. "Man on" or "Heads-up" will let the teammate know that pressure is being applied. A player may tell a teammate about to receive a ball to "turn" because there are no defenders nearby. As players mature, they will see that being a good communicator on the field can help the team win games.

To encourage verbal communication, set players up in a short-sided scrimmage. Ask them to talk to their teammates whenever they can. Award a point for every good tip spoken by one teammate to another. At the end, recognize the one player who provides the most verbal cues for teammates.

Stay in Shape

Soccer players are always on the go! There is no better way to train for soccer than to play the sport itself. That said, there are many other forms of exercise that are complementary to soccer and promote good health. In fact, most sports help athletes develop skills that are useful in soccer. Jogging, swimming, basketball and tennis are a few examples. For keepers, ping pong and air hockey help develop hand-eye coordination.

In soccer, a player moves at his or her own pace and each player has a particular work rate. Players who can run the most have a clear edge, especially late in the game when many players tend to wear down. Emphasize this point to players.

An Emphatic Message for Players: Keep Your Cool

Players perform at their best when they stay calm on the field, no matter what happens around them. Maintaining composure can sometimes be a challenge for even the calmest player. After all, there are many events that can happen on the field that might cause a player to become excited. Let's consider four examples.

A Player Thinks the Referee Made a Poor Call

If the referee makes a call that a player disagrees with, the player should forget about it and move on. Chances are that poor calls will even out during the course of the game. If a player becomes agitated, that player will lose focus and not play well. Remind players that the referee's decision is final. Any flak they give to the referee could haunt them later in the match, and may even cause them to be removed from the game. Players should always respect the referee.

An Opposing Player Calls a Player a Name

When an opposing player says something negative to a player, that player is trying to draw a response. If the player does respond, this means the player has been sucked into the trap and has lost concentration. Players should ignore any attempts to distract them from the game.

When the opponent draws no reaction from taunts, that player will have wasted energy. And once it becomes clear a player can't be rattled, the nonsense will likely stop.

A Player Becomes Angry at a Teammate Who Failed to Pass the Ball

The upset player should be trained not to approach the teammate directly. The teammate may take it personally and shun the player for the rest of the match. Instead, the player should know to tell you, the coach, about the situation. It is up to you to determine how best to handle disputes of this nature, always stressing team play when appropriate.

A Player Says the Other Team Is Cheating

Even players as young as age six will come off the field and tell you that, "Number eight keeps pushing everybody." If there is a referee, tell players to let the referee know. If it is the coaches who are refereeing the match, suggest to the opposing coach that all players be reminded to play by the rules, and in this case to keep their hands down. In addition, remind players to focus on their own game.

Table 7-1. Six Keys to Smart Play

⚽ Think fast, play fast
⚽ Move without the ball
⚽ See the whole field
⚽ Communicate
⚽ Stay in shape
⚽ Keep your cool

Chapter 8

Encourage Creativity

Too many young American players are starting on the wrong foot.

Even in soccer strongholds like California and New York, the approach to teaching players is often flawed. Inexperienced coaches mistakenly think of soccer as a highly structured sport, much like football, basketball or baseball. This approach stifles both the physical and cerebral development of the young player.

Many people who coach or administer soccer today grew up on strictly regimented sports that limit the creative input of the players. For example, football players carry out assignments on each play; the only player who can create is the one with the ball. In baseball, every fielder covers only a certain part of the field and the ball is "programmed" to go to one of four bases. In basketball, the point guard often calls a play and teammates follow the script.

Soccer is an entirely different game. Soccer flows more freely and unpredictably, with relatively few set plays or interruptions. Each time a player gets the ball, the player can do something new with it, going wherever the imagination leads.

Many people schooled in the traditional American sports fail to grasp the distinctive nature of soccer and treat the sport as any other. They know, for example, that basketball is played with five players and baseball with nine fielders, whether at age seven or 27. They then conclude that since professional soccer is played 11 a side, it should be that way for all ages.

That's a costly misjudgment. In fact, putting so many players on the field dooms any chance that soccer will be played. Young players surrounded by 20 of their peers have no room to run, dribble or pass. There is no time to think, no time to create.

Although 11 against 11 at age eight may be exercise, it's not soccer. It's clusterball.

In clusterball, players swarm over the ball in what looks like a roving rugby scrum. On occasion the ball squirts out, enabling a lucky player to have a free whack. That player, salivating at the chance, blasts the ball aimlessly down the field. The crowd cheers. The player is reinforced. No matter that the other team has the ball.

Many coaches try to eliminate clusterball by enlarging the field. But it doesn't work, because the scrum follows the ball. In fact, playing on a huge field exacerbates the problem by inviting young players to drive the ball great distances rather than to gain control, think and pass.

Soccer-savvy countries take a different approach. In Brazil, for example, kids play three or four a side until they are ten or even older, and on smaller fields better suited to their size and stamina. Each player touches the ball often. Each player learns to dribble, pass and shoot. Each player learns to make decisions with the ball. Each player plays soccer.

Let kids explore the game. Encourage them to tap their creative powers. Tell them to push the ball between an opponent's legs, to try that shot from a tight angle, to heel the ball backward to a teammate.

Urge them to watch high-level soccer on TV and in person. They will see how the best players in the world often do the unexpected with the ball. They will see players doing things they have never seen, they will experiment, and they will become more complete players.

Table 8-1. Dos

⚽ Do shoot from tight angles
⚽ Do try a heel pass
⚽ Do slip the ball through an opponent's legs

Above all else, let them play the game. They learn best by experimenting on the field during relatively unstructured play.

Finally, there are several "don'ts" for coaches to keep in mind as they work to tap the creative potential in players. Don't tell a defender only to defend. Don't say to a midfielder, "Don't cross that line." Don't tell a player to never dribble the ball. Don't tell a player to never pass backward.

Teach the basic techniques. Encourage your players to find creative ways to apply those techniques.

Table 8-2. Don'ts
✪ Don't tell a defender to only defend
✪ Don't tell a player never to dribble
✪ Don't tell a player to never pass backward

Chapter 9

Restarts

The ball will likely go out of play several times during a match. The game will stop briefly and the ball will have to be put back into play. These are called "dead-ball situations" or "restarts." Restarts include the opening kick-off, the kick to start the second half, corner kicks, goal kicks, free kicks and throw-ins.

To the untrained eye, restarts may look like a routine part of the game. But teams that learn how to execute them fast and with precision can gain a real advantage. In fact, many goals are scored after an effective restart.

Throw-ins

When the ball crosses the sideline, a throw-in is awarded to the team that did not touch the ball last. Teams that execute throw-ins well have a clear edge. Alert players can use a throw-in to get the ball to an open teammate or even set up a teammate for a shot at goal. There are three components to a good throw-in.

Form

The ball should be gripped firmly with fingers spread wide. The thumbs and index finger should be behind the ball. Arms are brought back, the back is arched and the knees are slightly bent. In one motion, the arms and the body come forward and the ball is released as it is brought over the head. The ball must fly straight out of the player's hands. The player must follow through with both arms and keep both feet flat on the ground (see illustration on p. 19).

Speed

Sometimes the opponent will pause to catch a breath when the ball goes out of bounds. A quick-thinking player can get the ball back into play before the opponent can react. Encourage players to see every throw-in as an opportunity to get the ball to an open teammate. When the other team is throwing the ball in, tell players to be alert and mark every player nearby.

Accuracy

When a teammate is open, the throw should be aimed at the receiving player's feet. The teammate can then control the ball easily and move quickly into open space. When a thrown ball comes to the player at the knee or above, the receiver must take time to bring it under control before moving ahead with it. This may enable a defender to close in and challenge for the ball.

The player throwing the ball should quickly get back into the game. The player may be able to find open space and even receive a return pass right away.

Table 9-1. Keys to a Good Throw-in

- ✪ Feet on the ground
- ✪ Knees bent
- ✪ Ball brought back behind head, arms moving together
- ✪ Follow through until hands are parallel to ground
- ✪ Get back in the game

Experienced players sometimes take a running start to get more distance on the throw. This can help a player throw the ball all the way into the middle of the field. Players using this approach should be reminded to keep both feet on the ground.

When It's Their Throw-in

Encourage players to run into open spaces toward the goal they are attacking. The thrower should throw the ball to the feet of an open teammate. If no teammate is open, the ball can be thrown down the sideline where a teammate can try to run onto it.

When the Other Team Gets a Throw-in

Encourage players to drop back and face the thrower. Players should mark all opponents nearest the thrower. They should try to anticipate where the throw will go and get there first.

Corner Kicks

Corner kicks result when the defending team last touches a ball that goes across the end line. The ball is placed in the corner of the field. As a player kicks the ball into play, all opponents must be at least ten yards away (see illustration on p. 21).

When It's Their Corner Kick

Young players play on narrow fields with short distances from the corners to the goalmouth. As a result, the corner kick can be a potent opportunity to score. Players should practice kicking the ball toward the area in front of the goal. Teammates should set up about ten or 15 yards away from the goal line, and should be scattered evenly through the goal box.

When the corner kick is made, the teammates should run from several different angles into the goal box and try to knock the ball in the goal.

When the Other Team Gets a Corner Kick

Teams need to be aggressive in defending against corner kicks. Encourage players to think that they must get to the ball first, whether the ball comes in the air or on the ground. A good move is to put your best defender just off the near post facing the corner. This defender is charged with clearing away any ball that comes in that direction.

Corner kicks often result in a mad scramble in front of the goal, with the ball bouncing perilously about the goal mouth. When this happens,

---

Table 9-2. Keys to a Good Corner Kick

- ⚽ Teammates move in front of the goal
- ⚽ Kicker sends the ball in front of the goal
- ⚽ Teammates attack the ball and shoot

---

defending players should focus on kicking the ball down the flanks of the field, away from danger. Under no circumstances should a defending player try to dribble the ball out of the goal area right after a corner kick. The risk of losing the ball and surrendering a score is too great.

Goal Kicks

A goal kick is taken when the ball goes across the end line after being touched last by an attacking player. The ball is placed along the line at the top of the goalie box, six yards from the end line of a regulation field. The goalie or a defender runs up and kicks the ball down the field (see illustration on p. 20).

In games played among players ages six through ten, the referee should instruct opposing players to back up at least 10 yards from the spot of the kick. However, do not count on this happening. Opposing players are often allowed to stand just a few yards away from where the ball is placed. This makes the goal kick an even more important part of the game.

When It's Their Goal Kick

Remind players that the goal kick is an opportunity to clear the ball and start the attack. First, focus on clearing the ball. Emphasize the need to keep the ball away from the front of your goal. It is best to have the ball kicked to the side of the field. It is ideal to have a player who can launch the ball into the air over any opponents who are standing nearby. It is a real bonus if a player can deliver a pass to a teammate near the closest sideline.

First, select one or two strong-footed players to take the goal kicks. Second, instruct the other players to run wide into open space and call for the ball if unmarked. As players grow, they will eventually be able to drive the ball clear, thus relieving the stress a coach can feel about goal kicks!

When the Other Team Has a Goal Kick

Instruct players to back up ten yards from the spot of the ball. It is best to give the other team room to put the ball back into play, rather than have your players cluster nearby. Instruct your players to spread wide across the field so you have a player ready to attack the ball no matter where it is kicked. Focus on regaining control after the kick and moving the ball back in front of the goal for a shot on net.

Table 9-3. Keys to a Good Goal Kick
☺ Play the ball wide
☺ Play the ball high
☺ Be first to the ball

Before a match, consider joining with the opposing coach and asking the referee to enforce the ten-yard rule throughout the game. This way, a dominant team has to work harder to score goals.

Free Kicks

Free kicks (see Law 13 in Chapter Two) are rare in games up through age 12. Even so, players should be prepared when they do happen.

When It's Their Free Kick

The objective with a direct kick depends on where the ball is. When the ball is in the third of the field closest to the goal being defended, the kicker should drive the ball up the field toward a teammate. When the ball is in the middle third, the kicker should look to pass to an open teammate who can ignite the attack. When the ball is in the attacking third, the kicker should launch the ball toward teammates in front of the opposing goal. When the kick is within 20 yards of the opposing goal, the best shooter should try a shot.

When the Other Team Has a Free Kick

Train players to move ten yards away from the ball. Make sure that players are spread evenly across the field, so they can defend effectively no matter where the ball is played. When the opposing kick can be placed near the goal they are defending, instruct players to be first to the ball and clear it to safe ground away from the goal.

Table 9-4. Keys to a Good Free Kick

⚽ Kicker plays the ball to an open teammate
⚽ Kicker drives the ball to teammates in front of
    the opposing goal
⚽ Kicker launches a powerful shot on goal

As players mature into their teens, they will be able to experiment with more elaborate direct kicks. For now, however, the focus should be on moving the ball toward the opposing goal.

Chapter 10

Running a Practice

Good practices can create a positive soccer experience for young players. In fact, most young players will learn more in practice than they will in games. Try to achieve four things in every practice.

First, educate players. Teach them something about soccer itself, be it a skill or a basic strategy. Teach them about the objectives of the game—to control the ball, to work the ball up the field, to create chances to score, and to keep the other team from creating chances to score. Make sure to emphasize the importance of good teamwork and fair play.

Second, stimulate and challenge players. Coaches who run the same drills and the same exercises practice after practice will cause players to lose interest. Give them something fresh to hold their excitement. Start practice with instruction on one of the fundamentals—passing, receiving, turning, controlling, shielding, shooting, heading and dribbling.

Introduce a drill or two that requires players to execute each such fundamental technique. Move to small-sided games where the focus continues on that technique. End the practice with a specific challenge. For example, have them juggle the ball five times with their feet. Remember to work them. They need to appreciate that effort has to go into the game.

Third, make sure that players are routinely praised and encouraged. When they do something well, let them know. Help them build confidence. A kind word goes a long way for young players who are working hard and making good progress.

Fourth, and most important, make sure the players have fun. When they have fun, they work hard, they learn and they grow. And coaches have fun too!

Table 10.1. Keys to a Good Practice

⚽ Teach your players something
⚽ Challenge them
⚽ Praise them
⚽ Make it fun

Length of Practices

For players ages five to seven, design practices to run about 45 minutes. That's a good stint for beginners.

For players eight to ten, practices should run about 60 minutes.

For players 11 and 12, practices can last as long as 90 minutes. No practices should last any longer than that.

Whatever length is chosen, keep it moving. Engage players. Long-winded speeches are counterproductive at these young ages.

The First Practice

It is important to establish a personal rapport with players at the beginning of the season. At the first practice, call the players together for introductions. Coaches should introduce themselves and give players a little background about their interest in soccer. Ask players to introduce themselves and talk about their experience in soccer.

Coaches should tell the players how they would like to be addressed ("Coach" or "Coach John" or whatever works best from the players' perspective.)

Coaches should tell players that their mission is to help them learn and enjoy soccer. As part of a coach's commitment to players, a coach should always be open to their questions and their ideas. This will help to put players at ease and lay the groundwork for a positive learning environment.

Stretching Exercises

Most young players will not want to spend a lot of time stretching. From the moment they get out of the car, they are ready to run.

That said, players should stretch before they start to play. Tell players to think of their body as a piece of bubble gum. When someone puts a wad of gum in their mouth, they can't blow a bubble right away, can they? They have to work the gum and loosen it up before they can blow a bubble. Now tell players to think of their bodies in the same way. They've got to be loose and limber before they can use their bodies.

Even the best-conditioned athletes should warm up before they take the field. It is generally recommended that players start with a light jog or brisk walk for five minutes or so. Another five minutes can be spent stretching all the parts of the body that will be used in the game.

Jogging and Walking

A light jog around the field will help the body get ready for competition. Jog forward and backward. While jogging, players should loosen their arms by swinging them gently in circles.

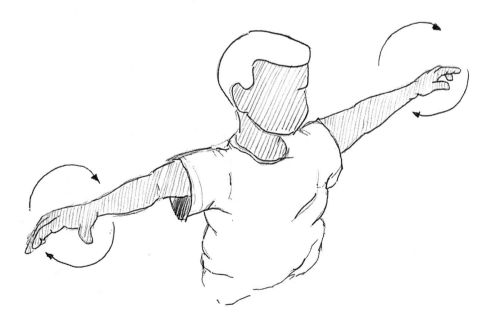

Figure 10-1. Jogging with Arms in Circles

Stretching with the Ball

One way to engage players in stretching exercises is to use a ball. This adds a new dimension and may help keep players focused on this important part of practice. There are many ways a ball can be used in stretching exercises.

Ball to the Ground

Each player holds a ball. Players stand with their legs about two feet apart. Legs are kept straight.

On the coach's command, the ball is brought down to touch the left foot. The player returns to an upright position. The player then reaches straight in front to touch the ball to the ground. After returning to the upright position, the player reaches to the right foot and then back up.

Figure 10-2. BALL TO THE GROUND

Ball to the Sky

Players hold the ball over their head with their arms straight. They gently lean in one direction with the ball, stretching the stomach muscles on the opposite side. They then reach with the ball in the other direction.

Figure 10-3. BALL TO THE SKY

Back to Back

Two players stand back to back. One player puts the ball over the head. The other player reaches up and takes the ball. The receiver then bends down and offers the ball back between the legs. The partner reaches down and collects the ball and then offers it over the head again.

Figure 10-4. BACK TO BACK

Round and Round

Two players stand back to back. The first player holds a ball, spins to the right and offers the ball. The partner spins to the left and takes the ball. That player then spins back to the right to offer the ball back, and the partner spins left to meet the player. This is a good way to loosen the muscles in the lower back.

Over the Top

This exercise is tricky. Four or five players lie on the ground, single file. One player at the end has the ball held between the feet. Upon the coach's command, the player picks the ball up with the feet, and brings

Figure 10-5. ROUND AND ROUND

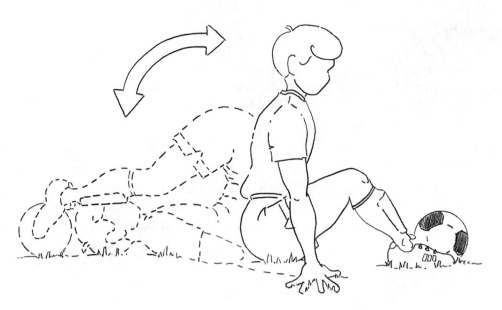

Figure 10-6. OVER THE TOP

the legs and the ball overhead. The player releases the ball on the ground behind the head and then brings the feet back over the head. The second player in line picks up the ball and does the same thing, until all players have used their feet to move the ball to the end of the line.

Sit-ups

Two players sit opposite each other with their feet meeting in the middle. One has a ball and lowers into sit up position, comes up and gives the ball to the teammate. The teammate then does a sit-up with the ball and returns it to the partner. Ten of these at each practice will do wonders to strengthen stomach muscles.

Figure 10-7. SOCCER SIT-UPS

Stretching Without the Ball

There are many other exercises without the ball that will help players get loose and avoid injury.

Ankle

While standing or sitting, the player lifts one foot off the ground and slowly draws a circle in the air with the toes, first in one direction and then the other. This is done with each foot.

Figure 10-8. ANKLE

Calf

The player places one foot about two feet behind the other, keeping the rear leg straight, and points both feet forward. The heels are kept on the ground. The player bends the forward leg until he or she feels a stretch in the back calf. The player holds that position for a few seconds and then changes positions with the legs.

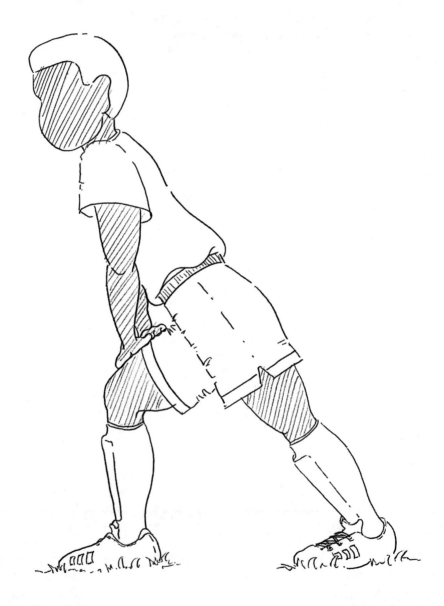

Figure 10-9. CALF

Groin

The player stands with feet wide apart and then bends one knee while keeping the other leg straight. The heels stay down. This stretches the muscles in the straight leg where the leg meets the waist. This is done with each leg. These muscles are used a great deal during a match when players run and kick.

Figure 10-10. GROIN

Back of Thigh

The player puts one leg out straight ahead and bends the other knee. The buttocks stay directly behind the player and the back is kept straight. The player leans forward until feeling a stretch in the back of the thigh of the straight leg. The player holds this for a few seconds and then does the same with the other leg.

Figure 10-11. BACK OF THIGH

Front of Thigh

The player stands on one leg and bends the other up behind. The player keeps the other knee slightly bent, and holds the free hand out for balance. The player grips the ankle and gently pulls the foot up. The player holds for a few seconds and then does the same with the other leg.

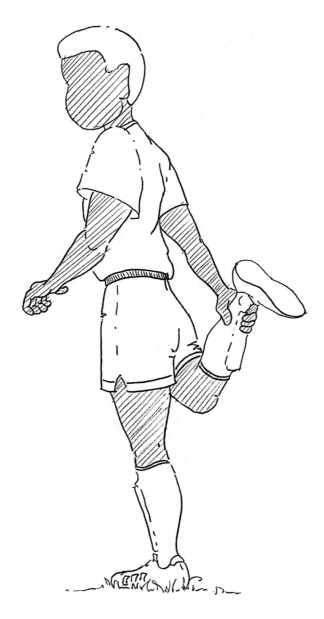

Figure 10-12. FRONT OF THIGH

Side Stretch

The player reaches up with one hand as high as possible and leans gently in the opposite direction. The player will feel a stretch down the side. The player holds for a few seconds and does the same on the other side.

Figure 10-13. SIDE STRETCH

Shoulder Stretch

The player lifts the shoulders up to the ears then lets them drop down. This is done a few times, slowly.

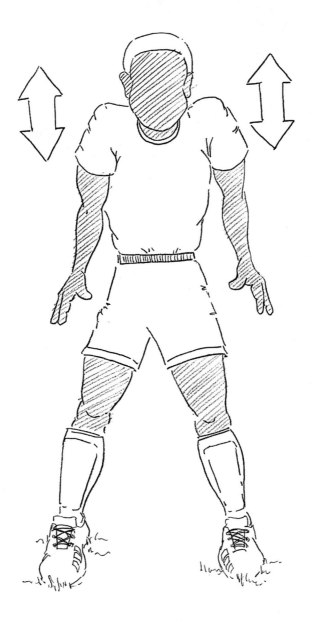

Figure 10-14. SHOULDER STRETCH

Head/Neck Stretch

The player pushes the forehead against the hand and stiffens the neck muscles. The player moves the head sideways against one hand. This is done in both directions. The player lowers the chin and rolls the head slowly from side to side. This loosens the neck muscles and prepares them for heading.

Structuring a Practice

For starters, make sure the right equipment is on hand. A good rule is to have a ball per player, 12 cones, six pinnies and a medical kit. Players should have their own balls and bring them to each practice and game.

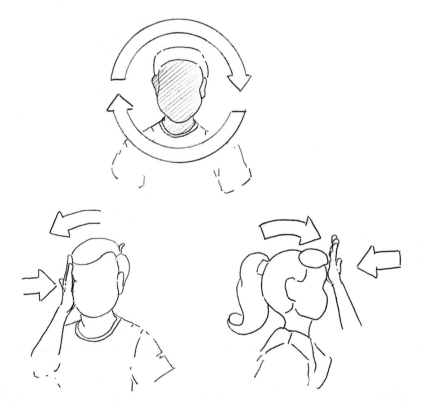

Figure 10-15. HEAD AND NECK STRETCH

Table 10-2. Equipment Checklist

- ☻ A ball per player
- ☻ 12 cones
- ☻ 6 pinnies
- ☻ Medical kit

A day or two before practice, try to spend 15 minutes thinking about what needs to be achieved in practice. Outline the flow on paper and bring it to practice. Arrive early if possible and do whatever set-up is necessary before players arrive. Always be ready to launch into practice as soon as players are there.

Many coaches prefer to build each practice around a single theme or technique, especially for players ages eight and up. They demonstrate the technique, have the players practice it, and then introduce drills that require the players to use the technique. Some common themes are dribbling, passing, shooting, controlling, turning and heading. Age appropriate sample practices are provided at the end of this chapter.

Go Easy on the Whistle

A key to effective coaching is knowing when to stop play to provide instruction or comment and when to let the players carry on. As a rule, the fewer times you stop play, the better. The kids learn best from playing. That said, if a player does something especially well—or if an opportunity to demonstrate a better way presents itself—stop the game, make the point quickly and let play resume. With time coaches will develop the instinct to interject only when it makes sense.

Asking Parents to Support the Team

Before the season starts, a coach should meet with all the parents in a single gathering. This will give them a chance to get to know both the coach and coaching philosophy. Coaches should tell about any interest and background they have in the sport. They should convey their interest in creating an experience that will be fun and educational for every player on the team.

Coaches should explain what they expect from the parents. They should ask for help. Ideally, someone will volunteer to serve as assistant coach. This person will help run the practice and manage the games. The assistant can help set up practice, oversee drills and provide encouragement to the players.

In time, the assistant coach may be able to run practices and games in the coach's absence. A coach, of course, should try to make every scheduled event, but chances are something will come up at least once or twice during the season. Having a strong assistant to lean on is very important.

There are many other tasks that must be undertaken to ensure a smooth season. Coaches should ask parents to help out in the following ways:

- provide snacks for halftime and after the games (players should bring water)
- provide a first aid kit, including ice packs for each game and practice
- confirm the time, location and referees for each match
- set up a phone chain used to alert parents to any changes in the schedule
- provide results to the sponsoring soccer club (travel soccer)
- record results and highlights and share them with the local paper (travel soccer)
- as needed, parents could volunteer to serve as linespeople when there is only one referee

A critical point: at the beginning of the season, tell the parents that players are expected to be on time for every practice and game. That means they arrive at practice at least five minutes early and at games at least 15 minutes early. Explain when practices and games will end and make sure that parents are there to pick up their kids. Coaches do not want to be standing around in the dark, waiting for the one parent who thought practice ended at 7:00, not 6:30.

Practice Tips for Players Ages Five to Seven

Among players ages five to seven, concentration spans are limited. At this age, every player will want to dribble the ball. It is too early to expect them to understand the concepts of passing and running into space.

As such, any game that involves more than three to a side is bound to result in "cluster soccer," which looks like a rugby scrum (see Chapter 8). For best results, keep games to no more than three to a side and introduce new drills frequently. Each player should get a good number of touches on the ball.

Table 10-3. The Practice Credo

☺ Tell me, I'll forget (too much talk causes players to tune out)
☺ Show me, I may remember (demonstrate, so players can see what is meant)
☺ Involve me, I'll understand (ask the players to try; they learn best this way)
☺ Perfect practice makes perfect (keep an eye on players; make sure the technique is right)

Sample Practices

Here are some sample practices, for players ages five to seven, eight to ten and 11 to 12. Drills are explained in the following chapter.

Ages Five to Seven

First Practice	*Minutes*
Introduce yourself	0:00
Ask players to introduce themselves	
Provide brief primer on rules	0:05
Light jog with ball around half the field (appoint a leader)	
Stretching—ball to the ground	0:10
Bulldog	0:20
Three x three (or four x four)	0:40
Final comments and observations (praise for hustle)	0:45

Second Practice	
Solicit questions about practice and games	0:00
Light jog with ball around half the field (appoint a leader)	
Stretching—ball to the sky	0:05
Foot boxing	0:10
Shark	0:20
Three x three (or four x four)	0:40
Final comments and observations	0:45

Third Practice

Solicit questions about practice and games	0:00
Light jog with ball around half the field (appoint a leader)	
Stretching—round and round	0:05
Tap dance	0:10
Policeman game	0:20
Three x three (or four x four)	0:40
Final comments and observations	0:45

Fourth Practice

Solicit questions about practice and games	0:00
Light jog with ball around half the field (appoint a leader)	
Stretching—soccer sit ups	0:05
Pairs passing	0:10
Red light, green light	0:20
Three x three (or four x four)	0:40
Final comments and observations	0:45

Fifth Practice

Solicit questions about practice and games	0:00
Light jog with ball around half the field (appoint a leader)	
Stretching—round and round	0:10
Footsie	0:20
Three x three (or four x four)	0:40
Final comments and observations	0:45

Sixth Practice

Solicit questions about practice and games	0:00
Light jog with ball around half the field (appoint a leader)	
Stretching—back to back	0:10
Crab alley	0:20
Three x three (or four x four)	0:40
Final comments and observations	0:45

Seventh Practice

Solicit questions about practice and games	0:00
Light jog with ball around half the field (appoint a leader)	
Stretching—ball to the sky	0:10
Musical soccer	0:20
Three x three (or four x four)	0:40
Final comments and observations	0:45

Eighth Practice

Solicit questions about practice and games	0:00
Light jog with ball around half the field (appoint a leader)	
Stretching—ball to the ground	0:10
Split the wicket	0:20
Three x three (or four x four)	0:40
Final comments and observations	0:45

Ninth Practice

Solicit questions about practice and games	0:00
Light jog with ball around half the field (appoint a leader)	
Stretching—round and round	0:10
Dribbling through cones	0:20
Three x three (or four x four)	0:40
Final comments and observations	0:45

Tenth Practice

Solicit questions about practice and games	0:00
Light jog with ball around half the field (appoint a leader)	
Stretching—soccer sit ups	0:10
Numbers game	0:20
Three x three (or four x four)	0:40
Final comments and observations	0:45

Ages Eight to Ten

First Practice

Introduce yourself	0:00
Ask players to introduce themselves	
Provide brief primer on rules	0:05
Light jog with ball around half the field (appoint a leader)	
Stretching—ball to the ground	0:10
Inside of foot pass—demonstrate	0:15
Pairs passing	0:25
Soccer marbles	0:35
Three x three (or four x four)	0:55
Final comments and observations (praise for hustle)	0:60

Second Practice

Light jog with ball around half the field (appoint a leader)	
Stretching–ball to the sky	0:10
Controlling pass with inside of foot–demonstrate	0:15
Pairs passing	0:25
Passing through cones	0:35
Three x three (or four x four)	0:55
Final comments and observations (praise for hustle)	0:60

Third Practice

Light jog with ball around half the field (appoint a leader)	
Stretching–round and round	0:10
Turning–the drag back–demonstrate	0:15
Turn and chase	0:25
Numbers game (points awarded for drag backs)	0:35
Three x three (or four x four)	0:55
Final comments and observations (praise for hustle)	0:60

Fourth Practice

Light jog with ball around half the field (appoint a leader)	
Stretching–over and under	0:10
Heading–demonstrate	0:15
Throw, head, catch	0:25
Heading game	0:35
Three x three (or four x four)	0:55
Final comments and observations (praise for hustle)	0:60

Fifth Practice

Light jog with ball around half the field (appoint a leader)	
Stretching–over and under	0:10
Dribbling–demonstrate inside, outside	0:15
Dribbling through cones	0:25
Bulldog	0:35
Three x three (or four x four)	0:55
Final comments and observations (praise for hustle)	0:60

Sixth Practice

Light jog with ball around half the field (appoint a leader)	
Stretching–soccer sit-ups	0:10

Tackling—demonstrate block, poke	0:15
1 v 1s between cones	0:25
Shark	0:35
Three x three (or four x four)	0:55
Final comments and observations (praise for hustle)	0:60

Seventh Practice

Light jog with ball around half the field (appoint a leader)	
Stretching—head and neck exercises	0:10
Shielding—demonstrate basics	0:15
1 v 1s in a small box	0:25
Pokeaway	0:35
Three x three (or four x four)	0:55
Final comments and observations (praise for hustle)	0:60

Eighth practice

Light jog with ball around half the field (appoint a leader)	
Stretching—ankle	0:10
Goalkeeping—demonstrate catching technique	0:15
Ball roll	0:25
Catching Circle	0:35
Three x three (or four x four)	0:55
Final comments and observations (praise for hustle)	0:60

Ninth Practice

Light jog with ball around half the field (appoint a leader)	
Stretching—calf	0:10
Dribbling—demonstrate inside, outside	0:15
Dribbling through cones	0:25
Find the line	0:35
Three x three (or four x four)	0:55
Final comments and observations (praise for hustle)	0:60

Tenth Practice

Light jog with ball around half the field (appoint a leader)	
Stretching—thigh	0:10
Shooting—demonstrate instep technique	0:15
One-Two shoot	0:25

Four goal free-for-all	0:35
Three x three (or four x four)	0:55
Final comments and observations (praise for hustle)	0:60

Ages 11-12

First Practice

Introduce yourself	0:00
Ask players to introduce themselves	
Light jog with ball around the field (appoint a leader)	0:05
Stretching—ball to the ground	0:10
Pairs passing	0:15
Two-lane highway	0:25
Break	0:30
Passing through cones	0:40
Two v One	0:50
Three x three (or four x four)	0:70
Final comments and observations (praise for hustle)	0:75

Second Practice

Light jog with ball around the field (appoint a leader)	0:05
Stretching—ball to the sky	0:10
Pairs passing	0:15
Passing to a circle	0:25
Break	0:30
Player in the middle	0:40
Five v two	0:50
Three x three (or four x four)	0:70
Final comments and observations (praise for hustle)	0:75

Third Practice

Light jog with ball around the field (appoint a leader)	0:05
Stretching—over and under	0:10
Pairs passing—left foot only	0:15
Footsie	0:25
Break	0:30
Cone attack	0:40
Four v one	0:50
Three x three (or four x four)	0:70
Final comments and observations (praise for hustle)	0:75

Fourth Practice

Light jog with ball around the field (appoint a leader)	0:05
Stretching—round and round	0:10
Juggling	0:15
Controlling—demonstrate inside of foot	0:25
Break	0:30
Pairs passing	0:40
Three v two plus a goalie	0:50
Three x three (or four x four)	0:70
Final comments and observations (praise for hustle)	0:75

Fifth Practice

Light jog with ball around the field (appoint a leader)	0:05
Stretching—shoulders	0:10
Juggling in pairs	0:15
Shielding—demonstrate technique	0:25
Break	0:30
Musical soccer	0:40
Three v two plus a goalie	0:50
Three x three (or four x four)	0:70
Final comments and observations (praise for hustle)	0:75

Sixth Practice

Light jog with ball around the field (appoint a leader)	0:05
Stretching—ankle	0:10
Juggling in pairs	0:15
Turning—demonstrate drag back	0:25
Break	0:30
Turn and chase	0:40
Footsie	0:50
Three x three (or four x four)—three touch	0:70
Final comments and observations (praise for hustle)	0:75

Seventh Practice

Light jog with ball around the field (appoint a leader)	0:05
Stretching—thigh	0:10
Juggling in pairs	0:15
Shooting—demonstrate instep	0:25
Break	0:30

Pairs passing—instep only, 20 yards apart	0:40
One—two shoot	0:50
Three x three (or four x four)—three touch	0:70
Final comments and observations (praise for hustle)	0:75

Eighth Practice

Light jog with ball around the field (appoint a leader)	0:05
Stretching—head and neck	0:10
Pairs passing—one touch	0:15
Heading—demonstrate	0:25
Break	0:30
Heading—back and forth	0:40
The heading game	0:50
Three x three (or four x four)—two touch	0:70
Final comments and observations (praise for hustle)	0:75

Ninth Practice

Light jog with ball around the field (appoint a leader)	0:05
Stretching—thigh	0:10
Pairs passing—one touch	0:15
You first, me second	0:25
Break	0:30
Cross the line	0:40
Four goal free-for-all	0:50
Three x three (or four x four)—two touch	0:70
Final comments and observations (praise for hustle)	0:75

Tenth Practice

Light jog with ball around the field (appoint a leader)	0:05
Stretching—calf	0:10
Pairs passing—one touch, left foot only	0:15
Footsie	0:25
Break	0:30
Players pick a drill	0:40
Players pick another drill	0:50
Full sided scrimmage	0:70
Final comments and observations (praise for hustle)	0:75

Chapter 11

Drills for Teams
and Individuals

Drills are an essential part of a good practice. They give players a way to develop their skills and learn the game. These activities must be fun and challenging and tailored for players.

The latter is absolutely critical—match the drills to the age of players. Appropriate drills will stimulate and educate a team. As players begin to master the basics, they will feel a sense of achievement that will carry them along to the next level. On the other-hand, drills that are beneath players may well cause them to become bored and lose interest. Drills that ask too much of players are likely to frustrate them and may cause them to question their abilities. Some age-based guidelines for what drills to use in practices follow.

Ages Five to Seven

Favor simple drills that require players to make frequent touches with the ball. At this age, the focus should be on controlling and dribbling the ball. Practice drills that call for simple tasks like dribbling the ball forward with the instep and moving the ball from side to side with the inside of the foot. Four fun games that help young players learn to play the ball are The Policeman Game, Bulldog, Shark and Red Light, Green Light (see the list that follows).

Ages Eight to Ten

By this age, many of your players will have developed the ability to control and move the ball. In addition to doing drills that reinforce controlling and dribbling, this is the right age to start engaging your players in passing drills. Some good basic passing drills for this age group include Passing Through Cones, Two-Lane Highway and Stuck in the Mud (see the list that follows).

Ages 11 to 12

At this age, engage your players in drills that mimic activity in a game. Drills should require that participants move the ball quickly, just as they must do in a game at this age. A good drill at this age is Four Corners, which requires four players to play keep-away from another player within a confined space such as a box 15 yards by 15 yards.

Here is a broad mix of drills designed to help your players develop and hone the basic skills of the game. The drills are broken down into team drills and individual drills. The skill drills for teams are: passing, dribbling, shooting, turning, heading, controlling, shielding, tackling and goalkeeping. There are also "game" drills (drills that mimic game activity) for teams. The skill drills for individuals are: controlling, dribbling, passing, shooting, shielding, turning, heading and goalkeeping.

Table 11-1. General Tips on Drills

- ☺ Combine conditioning, strategy and skill
- ☺ Get all players involved, so that no one is standing around
- ☺ Work a shooting drill into every practice
- ☺ Ask players to demonstrate
- ☺ Try to match kids of equal ability

Team Drills—Passing

All Ages

Back and Forth

Two players stand ten yards apart and pass the ball back and forth. Encourage players to use the inside of the foot to pass and control the ball. As players mature, they can "one-time" the ball back on softer passes. Instruct players to use each foot.

Benefit: This is a sound loosen-up drill at any age. It is also a good way for players to become comfortable receiving and kicking the ball.

Two-Lane Highway

Set up three cones in a row, four yards apart, creating two passing lanes separated by the center cone. Players stand six yards on either side of the cones. One player passes the ball through one lane. The receiver controls the ball in the direction of the other lane and returns a pass through that lane. Each player touches the ball twice on each possession; once to control and a second time to pass. Players cannot pass the ball back through the lane in which they received it.

Benefit: This drill mimics what often happens in a game. Players focus on controlling the ball into space, away from an oncoming opponent. It also encourages them to pass the ball soon after they possess it. Finally, the drill focuses players on the need to make an accurate pass.

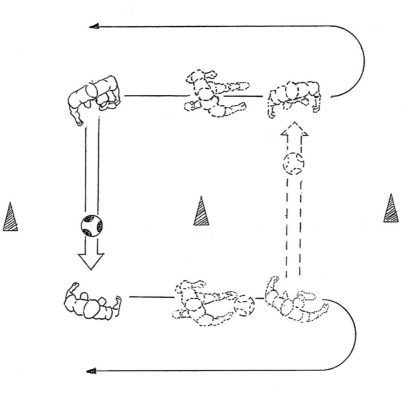

Figure 11-1. Two-Lane Highway

Ages Eight to Ten

Passing Through Cones

Put six cones five yards apart from each other in a straight line. Move 20 yards across the field and lay cones down at the same intervals as you work your way back to the line that you started from. Players pair up, with each starting two yards on either side of the first cone. The players move forward, passing the ball back and forth between the cones as they go. When they get to the end of the first row, they dribble over to the next row of cones and work their way back to the starting point.

Encourage players to lead their teammates, playing the ball a few yards ahead so the teammate can run comfortably onto it. Ask players to try to one-time each ball, rather than control and then pass. The emphasis is on soft, accurate passes.

Benefit: This drill focuses players on making accurate passes with a rolling ball, a skill that will serve them well in games.

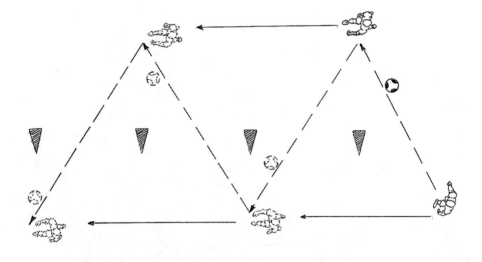

Figure 11-2. Passing Through Cones

Stuck in the Mud

Two teams of five play in a box 15 yards by 15 yards. Players on the white team have balls, players on the yellow team do not. White team players try to hit yellow team players with passes. When a yellow team player is struck below the knee, that player has to stand still with his legs apart and say, "stuck in the mud." That player must remain this way until a teammate crawls between the player's legs to free him. When the white team freezes all five opponents, the teams switch rolls.

Benefit: This drill helps young players work on accuracy in their kicks. It also encourages teamwork.

Two Versus One

Two attackers start near one end of a rectangle 20 yards by 8 yards, while a defender starts at the other end. The defender passes the ball to the attackers, who try to work the ball, under control, past the defender and across the far line. Encourage the attackers to pass the ball. Encourage the defender to force the attacker to pass.

Benefit: This drill focuses the attackers on working together to move the ball down the field. Players learn to rely on their teammate to move the ball effectively ahead. The defender, meanwhile, learns to position himself so that the attacking players must work together to beat him.

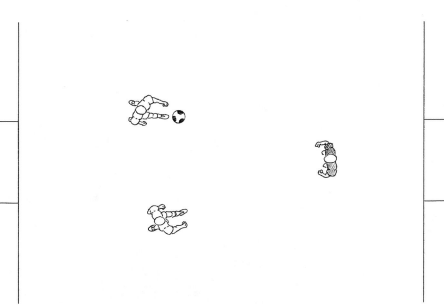

Figure 11-3. TWO VERSUS ONE

Ages 11 to 12

Passing to a Circle

One player has the ball at his feet, the rest (four to five others) jog around him in a circle about 20 yards in diameter (like the center circle of a regulation soccer field). The player in the center calls the name of one of the jogging players. He then serves a pass to that player, aiming the ball a few feet in front so the receiver naturally runs onto it. The player receiving the ball then dribbles into the middle and calls out the name of the next receiver. When players keep the ball moving quickly, everyone gets a good number of touches.

Benefits: This drill promotes teamwork and challenges players to receive a moving ball when they are on the run.

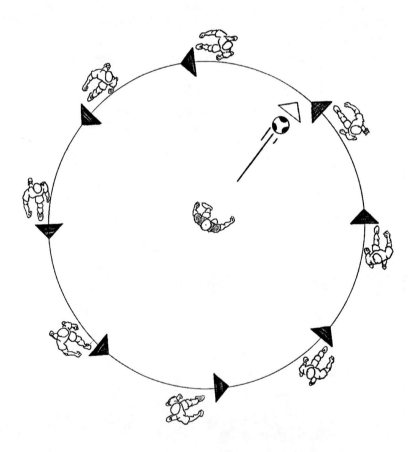

Figure 11-4. PASSING TO A CIRCLE

Four Corners

Four players stand in the corners of a square about ten yards by ten yards. They pass the ball among themselves while another player tries to intercept. Each player takes a turn in the middle.

Benefit: This drill forces the players in the corners to play the ball quickly when under pressure. The player in the middle enhances his tackling drills and works on his endurance.

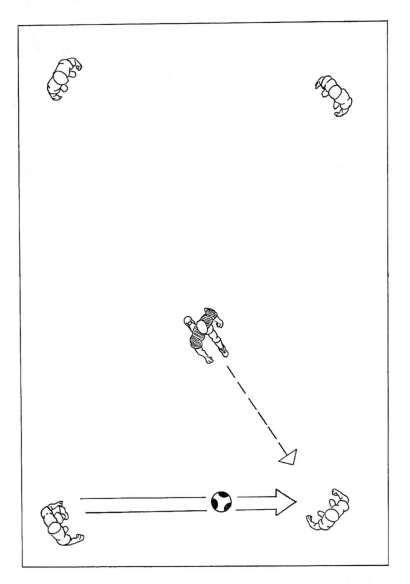

Figure 11-5. FOUR CORNERS

Player in the Middle

One player stands in the middle of the square with four players positioned around the outside of the square, one on each side. Two of the four outside players have balls, two do not. A player on the outside throws a ball to the player in the middle. That player controls it and passes it to one of the players without a ball, but not to the player who threw it. The player in the middle focuses on controlling the ball in the direction he plans to pass it.

Benefit: This drill focuses the receiving player to think about what to with the ball before he possesses it. This is a wonderful ability at any age. The drill also challenges the player in the middle to control and pass the ball.

Five Versus Two

Five players try to keep the ball from two players in a box about 20 yards by 20 yards. The team of five wins a point each time it completes five straight passes; the team of two gets a point for taking the ball away. Players rotate after a few minutes.

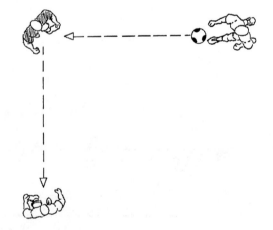

Figure 11-6. PLAYER IN THE MIDDLE

Figure 11-7. FIVE VERSUS TWO

Benefit: This drill mimics game activity, where one team often has a numerical advantage over the other in a confined space. This gives the team of five players a chance to touch the ball often and make decisions with the ball. It forces the team of two to work hard in pursuit of the ball.

Team Drills—Dribbling

All Ages

Footsie

Put players in a circle 15 yards in diameter, each with a ball. On the whistle, ask the players in the circle to dribble around within the circle. After a minute, ask them to use only the inside or outside of one foot. After another minute, ask them to use only the left foot. After another minute, instruct them to use only the sole of the foot. They then go back to using all parts of both feet. On the sound of the whistle, they must stop quickly. On the next whistle, they burst to top speed.

Benefit: This drill encourages players to use all parts of the foot in dribbling the ball. It also challenges players to keep their heads up as they move about in crowded spaces.

One Versus One

Set up two cones about six yards apart. Starting ten yards away, players take turns trying to dribble the ball around each other and through the cones.

Benefit: Players work on two fundamental skills: dribbling and tackling. Make sure to match players of even ability in this drill. An inferior player will quickly become discouraged.

Box Dribble

Put six to eight players with their balls into a box about 15 yards by 15 yards. Expand the area for older players. Players try to knock the other balls out of the box while keeping possession of theirs. Players whose balls go out of the box retrieve them and return to the game. This can be done in a circle as well.

Benefit: Players are forced to think about possessing their own ball while trying to dispossess another player at the same time. All at once, players work on their shielding, dribbling and tackling abilities.

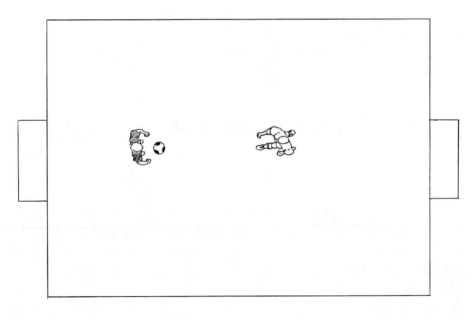

Figure 11-8. ONE VERSUS ONE

Find the Line

Players start near the middle of a lined square with the ball at their feet. When the coach yells, "find the line," players have to dribble the ball and stop it right on one of the lines. The last player to do so is eliminated. Continue until there is a winner. After a few rounds, scatter four or fives cones through the square. Players whose balls hit a cone are also eliminated.

Benefit: This drill encourages players to dribble with speed while maintaining control of the ball. Players also work on controlling a moving ball.

Ages Five to Seven

Red Light, Green Light

Players spread a few yards apart with a ball at their feet and follow the directions of the coach in front of them. "Green light" means dribble forward, "yellow light" means slow down, "red light" means stop. Introduce gears to encourage changes of speed.

Benefit: This is a good way to help young players learn to dribble.

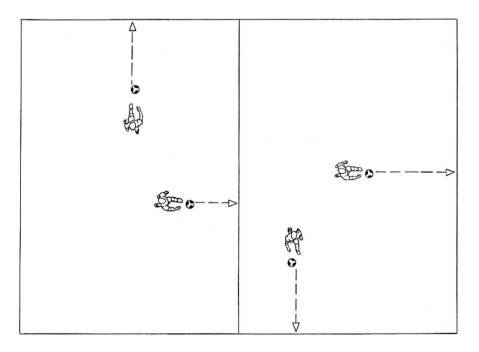

Figure 11-9. FIND THE LINE

Crab Alley

Mark an alley five yards wide by 30 yards long. Put two cones at each seven-yard interval. A "crab" defends each set of cones. The crabs are tummy up, on hands and feet. They can move only sideways between the cones.

A player starts at one end and tries to dribble around the crabs and through the cones. The crabs try to kick the ball away. They may not use hands.

Benefit: The dribbler learns to dribble the ball at an angle. The crabs improve their arm and leg strength.

Ages Eight to Ten

Bulldog

All but two players stand with balls at the end of a box 15 yards wide by 30 yards long. The other two players, or bulldogs, stand in the middle of the box. On the whistle, players try to dribble past the two bulldogs to the other end of the box. The bulldogs try to knock balls out of the box. Players whose balls leave the box become bulldogs. The game continues until the last player's ball goes out of the box.

Benefit: Players work on their dribbling skills. They must keep their heads up so they avoid the bulldogs. The drill also encourages dribblers to change speeds on occasion. The bulldogs practice their tackling skills.

Shark Attack

Two players start in the goal, without balls. The rest start with a ball at their feet, scattered through a box about 20 yards by 30 yards (the

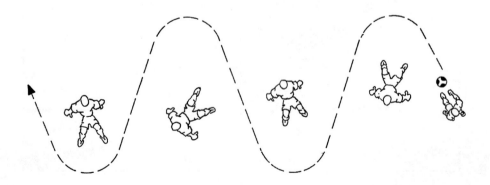

Figure 11-10. CRAB ALLEY

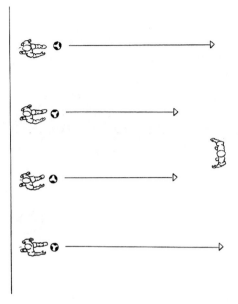

Figure 11-11. BULLDOG

penalty area works well on a regulation-size field). On the whistle, the two "sharks" come out and try to kick the balls out of the lined area. The other players must stay within the lines while avoiding the sharks. When a player's ball goes over the line, that player is eliminated. The last player remaining is the winner.

Benefit: Players work on their shielding and dribbling. Sharks work on pursuit and tackling.

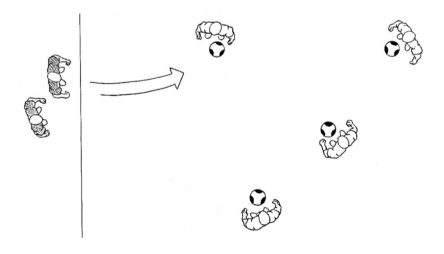

Figure 11-12. SHARK ATTACK

Musical Soccer

Put up to ten players in a box 20 yards by 20 yards. Seven players have a ball, three do not. The three players without a ball attempt to tackle the ball away from one of the seven who do. Each player tries to have possession of a ball when the coach periodically blows the whistle, say every 15 seconds. The three who do not should start the next round with a ball.

Benefit: Players must focus on dribbling and shielding while they have the ball, and on pursuit and tackling when they do not.

Split the Wicket

Put up to ten players in a box 15 yards by 15 yards. All have a ball except three, who stand with legs apart across the box. The seven dribblers move around the box, knocking the ball through the legs of the standing three and picking up the dribble on the other side. Players rotate every few minutes.

Benefit: This drill encourages players to keep their heads up as they move around the field. They also work on their dribbling and passing. While the three "standers" are immobile, they enjoy being the center of attention!

Square Dance

Mark a square 15 yards by 15 yards. Each player begins by dribbling the ball. Give instructions as follows: "Stop." Players put foot on top of the ball and freeze. "Go." Players move right or left with the ball quickly

Figure 11-13. MUSICAL SOCCER

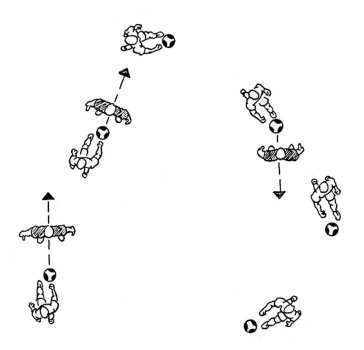

Figure 11-14. SPLIT THE WICKET

for five yards. "Turn." Players do an about-face quickly with the ball and move ahead for five yards. Players must stay within the marked area. They should try to avoid contact with other players or other balls.

Benefit: Players practice many techniques in this drill—dribbling, turning, controlling and shielding. They also must keep their heads up so they avoid running into one another.

Ages 11 to 12

You First, Me Second

Two players get together with one ball. They stand at one end of a rectangle about ten yards by 20 yards. One player dribbles the ball the length of the area, turns and dribbles it back to his teammate. The teammate repeats the drill while the first player rests. Have the players experiment with different turns each time, with an emphasis on touching the ball just once when they change direction at the other end.

Benefit: This drill enhances dribbling and turning skills and encourages players to dribble with speed.

Team Drills—Shooting

All Ages

One Versus One

One player starts dribbling in 30 yards from the goal, against a defender ten yards away. The player tries to beat the defender and launch a shot at goal.

Benefit: This imitates a basic sequence in games; take on a defender and shoot.

Ages Five to Seven

Me to You

Players stand about three yards apart. One player rolls a slow ball toward the other, who, toes pointed to the ground, kicks the ball gently back. Each player does this ten times before rotating.

Benefit: This simple exercise is a good way to help young players learn how to use their instep. With practice, they will learn to favor their instep to drive the ball low and hard.

Ages Eight to Ten

One-Two Shoot

Players line up 20 yards from the goal. Another player lines up five yards closer to the goal and ten yards off to the side. The player at the top passes to the player on the side who passes back to, but ahead of, the first player. The first player runs onto the pass and one-times a shot at goal from about 15 yards.

Benefit: This drill reinforces the importance of teamwork. It gives the shooter practice at striking a moving ball. The passer works on delivering a soft, short pass that can be easily struck.

Ages 11 to 12

Four Corner Firing Range

The shooter stands five yards beyond the top of the penalty box, next to a cone, facing the goal. A player stands in each corner of the penalty box with a ball. On the whistle, the shooter jogs around the cone as one of the two players at the top of the box passes the ball along the

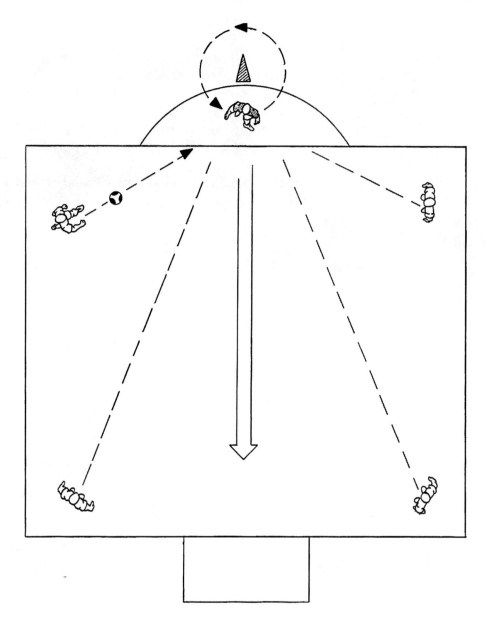

Figure 11-15. FOUR CORNER FIRING RANGE

18-yard line. The shooter runs onto the ball, shoots and then heads back around the cone. When he comes to the 18, he strikes the next ball played there. He continues until he has hit all four balls.

Benefit: Players learn how to shoot balls coming at them from different angles. They are encouraged to strike the ball with each foot. They also practice shooting while tired.

Cone Attack

Set up a box about 20 yards by 20 yards. Along opposite ends, place five cones about four yards apart. Four players play in each half of the box. Feed ball after ball into the box, alternating feeds between the teams. Try to keep two or three balls in play at once. The players try to knock down all the cones on the far end while defending the cones behind them from shots made by the other team. The first team to knock down all the cones wins.

Benefit: Players must think fast so they can launch shots and defend at the same time. This drill helps players work on their passing touch.

50 Kicks

A player stands a few yards in front of a net (a field hockey net is ideal). The player blasts the ball off the net, lets it bounce once and then drives it again. This is done 25 times in a row with each foot.

Benefit: This is a great way for a player to build leg strength and put power and accuracy into shots. This can be done during practice or on a player's own time.

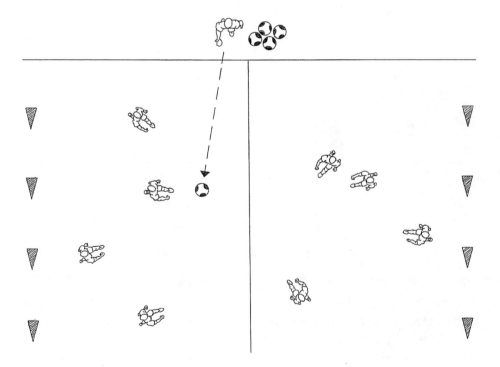

Figure 11-16. Cone Attack

Rebound!

Set up two lines facing the goal, each 15 yards off the posts. The coach stands in the middle, 15 yards from goal. The player at the front of the shooting line passes to the coach, who lays the ball off to the side so the shooter can run up and one-time the ball toward the inside of the far post. As the shooter strikes the ball, the player in the other line runs hard toward the far post. That player is there to knock in any rebounds that may be given up by the keeper. Ask the keeper to periodically roll a few saves back toward the rebounder, to keep everyone engaged.

Benefit: This drill focuses the shooter on the far post and the non-shooter on crashing the goal for a possible rebound opportunity.

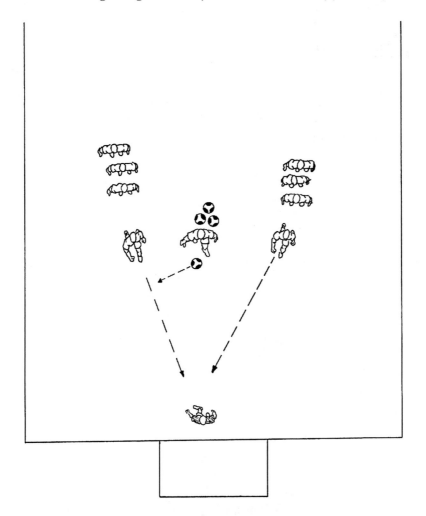

Figure 11-17. REBOUND!

Team Drills—Turning

All Ages

Turn and Chase

One player dribbles toward a teammate who stands 15 yards away. When the dribbler gets within three yards of the teammate, the dribbler puts a foot on top of the ball, drags it back in the other direction, turns and heads toward the starting point. As soon as the teammate sees the dribbler's back, the teammate chases the dribbler to the other line.

Benefit: Players learn how to turn and control the ball while moving at high speed under pressure. Defenders pursue and tackle.

Ages Eight to Ten

Cross the Line

Players line up on a line facing another line ten yards away. When the whistle sounds, the players dribble just beyond the line ten yards away, turn and dribble back across the original line. Ask them to do this twice, so they turn three times and cover 40 yards in total.

Benefit: This drill forces players to dribble with speed but also control. It also enhances their turning ability.

Three-Person Turn

Set up an area 20 yards by ten yards. Put one player at each end and one in the middle. The player at one end sends the ball to the player in the middle. That player receives the ball, turns and passes to the player at the other end. Give the player in the middle ten balls before changing positions.

Benefit: The players on the end work on their passing and receiving. The player in the middle works on controlling, turning and passing. This drill also promotes teamwork.

"Man-on" or "Turn"

Two players stand 15 yards apart. One player passes to the other. As the ball nears the receiver, the passer yells "man-on" or "turn." If the passer yells "man-on", the receiver one-times the ball back to the passer. If it's "turn," the receiver brings the ball under control and turns quickly up the field before turning around and preparing to deliver the ball back to his teammate.

Benefit: This drill encourages players to communicate on the field. It also enhances passing and turning skills.

Team Drills—Heading

There are four key points for all players to think about when heading the ball. Use the forehead. Keep eyes open. Keep mouth closed. Lean into the ball upon contact.

Ages Five to Seven

In-Line Heading

The coach stands five yards from players who stand in a line. The coach lobs the ball into the air. The first player steps forward and leans his forehead into the ball, sending it back toward the coach's chest. The player moves to the end of the line. Coach continues until each player has three or four chances.

Benefit: This is a safe, effective way to introduce heading to young players. Once your players do this drill a few times, they will begin to feel comfortable playing the ball with their heads.

Ages Eight to Ten

Throw-Head-Catch

Three players stand in a triangle. The first player throws the ball, the second heads it and the third catches it. Players do this in one direction for a minute or so and then reverse direction.

Benefit: This is another safe way for more experienced players to head the ball. This is an especially effective drill because all three players are engaged in every play.

Heading Down the Field

A player holds the ball, facing a teammate five yards away. The player throws the ball to the teammate, who heads it back. The thrower backpedals and continues to toss balls to the teammate as the teammates jogs forward. The players try to maintain about five yards between them. After the ball is headed 20 times, the players turn around and reverse roles. Advanced players can try to dribble another ball forward while doing the heading.

Benefit: This gives players an opportunity to head the ball while they are in motion, as is often the case in games.

Ages 11 to 12

Back and Forth

Players pair up and stand five yards apart from one another. They try to head the ball back and forth without letting it hit the ground.

Benefit: A game for more advanced players; see how many times in a row players can head the ball before it hits the ground.

Heading Game

Set up two goals, 30 yards apart. Divide the players into two teams. Players advance the ball by throwing it to teammates, who must catch it before it hits the ground. Players may take only one step after they catch the ball. If the ball is intercepted or touches the ground, the other team gets possession at that spot. A goal can be scored only with the head. As soon as the player with the ball gets close to the goal, teammates should make runs toward the goal. The player with the ball should look to set up a teammate for an easy header between the posts.

Benefit: Young players enjoy this combination of basketball and soccer. They learn to move without the ball so they can receive a pass from a teammate. They learn to look up when they get the ball because they themselves cannot advance it. And scoring a goal is a real kick because it requires a well placed head ball.

Team Drills—Controlling the Ball

Feet

Most of the dribbling and passing drills are also effective controlling drills because they require that players control the ball first. When running dribbling or passing drills, ask players to focus on controlling the ball effectively. Keep watch on how they do, and provide instruction as appropriate, in addition to focusing on dribbling and passing.

Thigh

Two teammates stand seven yards apart. They take turns tossing soft, arcing balls toward each other's waist. Throws should be made underhanded to create the lob. The receiver lifts a thigh as the ball nears and tries to "catch" the ball in the middle of that thigh. The player relaxes the raised leg as the ball lands. The ball will drop at the player's feet, where it can be played right away.

This drill can be done starting at age seven.

Benefit: This is a safe way for young players to learn how to use the thigh.

Chest

Players follow the same principle as with the thigh, only the ball is lobbed toward the chest. Players lean back and land the ball on the top of the chest, sagging back as the ball nears to cushion it. Again, the ball will fall to the player's feet.

Benefit: Again, this is a safe way to introduce the use of the chest to young players.

Team Drills—Shielding

Many of the dribbling and passing drills listed in this section will give players the chance to work on their shielding drills. Here's one shielding drill that is useful for players seven and older.

One versus One

Within a square ten yards by ten yards, give the ball to one player and ask another to take it away. Make sure the players stay within the square. When the defender has won the ball twice, switch positions.

Benefit: This is a great way for players to develop the basic skills of shielding, turning and tackling. It is also a good test of stamina and staying power.

Team Drills—Tackling

All Ages

Poke-Away

Each player starts with a ball inside a 20 yard by 20 yard square. Each player dribbles a ball within the square, while at the same time trying to kick someone else's ball out of the square. Players drop out of the game when their ball leaves the square. The last player left is the winner.

Benefit: A good primer for tackling, dribbling, shielding and turning.

Ages Eight to Ten

One versus One

Set up an area 20 yards long by ten yards wide. One player has the ball, while the other faces from three yards away. The player with the ball, staying inside the 10-yard width, tries to get past the opponent. The opponent tries to tackle the ball away.

Benefit: This is a useful drill for both players. The attacker practices dribbling, faking and accelerating with the ball, while the defender practices tackling skills.

Ages Eight and Up

Stop the Shooter

An attacker starts with the ball 25 yards from the goal. Two cones are placed 15 yards apart, 15 yards from the center of the goal. A defender

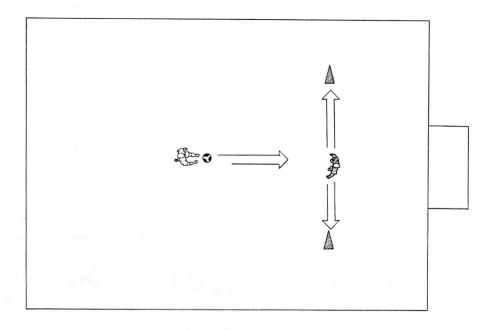

Figure 11-18. STOP THE SHOOTER

starts at one cone. As the attacker moves forward the defender moves across the imaginary line between the two cones. The defender can move sideways, but may not move forward or backward. The defender tries to tackle the attacker, who tries to get past the defender and launch a shot at goal.

Benefit: This drill tests the shooter's ability to accelerate past a stationary defender and to shoot under pressure. The defender tests his tackling skills.

Other Skill Drills—Volleying

Ages Eight and Up

Volleying

Players stand three yards apart. One player lobs a ball to the other, who kicks it out of the air back to the thrower. Rotate after six kicks.

Benefit: This is a simple introduction to kicking the ball out of the air. Players should use their instep for this kick, with the toe pointed toward the ground when contact is made.

Volleying

A player stands ten yards from goal. The player tosses the ball head-high and kicks it on the way down (volley). Then the player drops the ball and strikes it right after it bounces (half-volley).

Benefit: This helps players learn how to play balls that come in at unusual angles. This is a good skill to master, because sometimes there is no room on the field to do anything but one-time a ball out of a crowd.

Team Drills—Game Situations

All Ages

The Numbers Game

Mark an area about 25 by 35 yards. At opposite ends, use cones to set up goals five yards apart. Put an even number of players on each team, starting between the goalposts. Each player on each team is assigned a number, so, for example, each team of five has players numbered one to five. Stand on the side at midfield with several balls. Call out a number and kick a ball into play. The two players with the assigned number go for the ball and try to score in the opposing goal.

Players whose numbers are not called defend their goals, using feet only. If a ball goes out of play quickly, put another one back into play. Call one number, two or three. Mix it up for variety and to give adequate rest time between each "game," which should last no more than 45 seconds.

Benefit: This is a fun game that pits teammates in spirited competition. It builds camaraderie too, as the players in goal cheer on their teammates on the field.

Ages Eight to Ten

Four-goal Free-for-all

Goals four feet wide are set up on each side of a square 20 yards by 20 yards. Eight players play four against four, with each team trying to score into any of the four goals. There are no goalies.

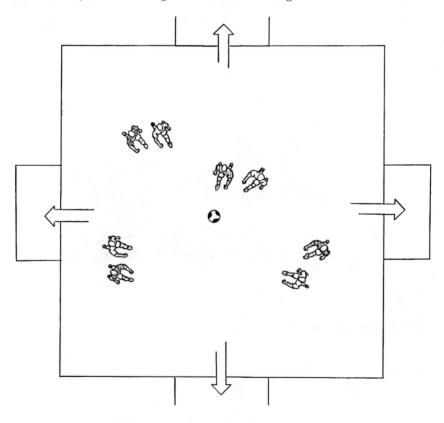

Figure 11-19. FOUR-GOAL FREE-FOR-ALL

Benefit: This game teaches players to think about moving in different directions with the ball. It also encourages them to attack the goal.

Age Eight and Up

Three versus Two Against a Keeper

Three players start 25 yards from the goal. Two defenders face them ten yards from the goal. The coach rolls a ball to the central attacker. The attackers attempt to work the ball past the defenders for a shot at goal.

Benefit: This drill imitates what often happens in a game. The attacking team tries to exploit its advantage. The defenders must work together to negate their disadvantage.

One versus One versus One

Three players stand together 15 yards from the goal. The coach throws the ball in from the sidelines. The players compete for possession, try to spring free and launch a shot at goal. The keeper gives the ball back to the coach, who continues to serve balls until the three players need a break. Stress the need to shoot when the opportunity arises.

Benefit: This drill fosters many important skills. Players learn how to scrap for a loose ball. They are challenged to dribble quickly into space and launch a shot. This game also shows players how quickly opponents can shut down a scoring chance.

Two-Touch

Set up a small-sided game in which players can touch the ball only twice each time they have possession.

Benefit: This forces players to keep the ball moving. It also puts the emphasis on the pass rather than the dribble. Finally, it encourages players to run to space to support a teammate, who has no option but to pass.

Three-Touch

Set up a small-sided game in which players can touch the ball only three times each time they have possession.

Benefit: Same as for two-touch.

Ages 11 to 12

Three versus One in a Box

In an area 15 yards by 15 yards, three players try to keep the ball from one player. The three players are encouraged to move into space for one another; the one defender is encouraged to keep putting pressure on the ball until a mistake is made.

Benefit: The three players must play the ball quickly and move into space, two important skills. The defender must pursue aggressively and tackle effectively.

Two versus One Plus Keepers

Set up an area about 20 yards by ten yards. Put goals at each end. Two players play against one player, with a keeper defending for each team. Make sure to rotate so that each player experiences playing alone and with a teammate.

Benefit: This game reflects what often happens in a match. Encourage the team of two to spread out and pass the ball effectively. Encourage the single player to try to force the player into a pass that he can intercept. Do not interrupt. Put a new ball into play when one goes out. Rotate every minute or so. After the drill—about ten minutes—ask players what they learned, both on offense and on defense.

One-Touch

Set up a small-sided game in which players can touch the ball only once each time they have possession.

Benefit: This game encourages players to think what they will do with the ball before they receive it. They focus on passing and moving without the ball.

Drills for Individuals

Ages Eight and Up

Juggling

A player throws the ball into the air, about as high as his head, and lets it bounce once. The player sees how many times the ball can be kicked before it hits the ground. This can be done alone or in a group.

Benefit: This is a good way for players to refine their touch. As players mature they can also use their head, chest and thighs. Asking them to try to beat their record provides extra motivation.

Foot Boxing

Players knock the ball back and forth between their feet as many times as they can in 20 seconds, without losing control.

Benefit: This simple drill improves foot speed and ball control. Again, encourage players to beat their record.

Bunny Hop

Players place the ball on the ground in front of them. They hop over the ball with both feet and then hop backward to where they started. They do this as many times as they can in 20 seconds.

Benefit: This drill increases foot speed and jumping ability. Encourage players to top their record.

Tap Dance

Players put the ball in front of them and tap the top of it with one foot and then the other. They do this for 20 seconds, trying to tap the ball as lightly as they can.

Benefit: This is another easy way for players to improve their feel for the ball.

Dribbling Through Cones

Put about six cones five yards apart from each other in a straight line. Players weave their way through the cones from one end to the other, using the insides and outsides of both feet. Tell them to go slowly at first.

Figure 11-20. DRIBBLING THROUGH CONES

They should try to keep the ball close by and look up every now and then. Once they're comfortable, put a stopwatch on them and encourage them to beat their best time.

Benefit: This drill will improve ball control and dribbling abilities. Players learn to move the ball across and away from their bodies.

Cut Left, Cut Right

This is a simple drill but a valuable one. Standing behind a still ball, players practice moving it forward in one of four different ways—with the inside of each foot and the outside of each foot. When the whistle is blown, say "outside of left foot," and they touch the ball three consecutive times with that part of the foot. Do this with each of the four options.

Benefit: Over time, players will become adept at all four of these movements and will be comfortable moving the ball in any direction. Players who are able to move the ball in this manner are far more difficult to defend.

Ages 11 to 12

Zig-Zag

To develop the outside of the foot, players move the ball in a zig-zag motion. They push the ball to the left with the outside of the left foot. Then they bring the right foot behind the ball and use the outside to move the ball back across the body. Players should go slowly at first. Speed is not important, technique is.

Benefit: This helps players become comfortable using the outside of each foot.

Heel Pass

The player dribbles forward and stops the ball to the side of the feet. The player swings the foot farthest from the ball in front of the other foot and knocks the ball with that heel straight backward.

Benefit: This bit of trickery will give players another way to play the ball backward.

Inside and Outside

The player places one foot on top of the ball. The player rolls the ball to the side until the foot touches the floor. Now the player goes back the other way until the foot touches the floor on the other side. This is done with each foot. The foot should always touch the ball.

Benefit: This simple drill helps players improve their touch. A good warm-up drill.

Drag Back

The player dribbles the ball across the field. With the ball slightly ahead, the player puts one foot on top, stops the ball and rolls it back in the other direction.

Benefit: This is an effective way to change directions with the ball.

Dash Dribble

Players start at the end of the field with a ball. They run with the ball at their feet as fast as they can for 50 yards, or to midfield. They keep the head up when not touching the ball. Instruct them to use the outside of the foot; it's the most natural way to move the ball forward while running.

Benefit: This will help players exploit space on the pitch. Being able to control the ball while running is a critical skill, especially for forwards.

Goalkeeper Drills

Focus young keepers on catching and throwing first. Once young players learn to catch and throw, they can focus on diving for the ball.

All Ages

Ball Roll

Players pair off, five to six yards apart, each standing between cones about four yards apart. They take turns rolling the ball, underhanded, on the ground to each other. You stress the proper technique for catching the ball: legs together, bend at the knees, collect the ball with arms together and fingers facing the ground. Once the ball is in hand, it is brought tight to the body.

Benefit: This is a good way to help players understand how to position themselves for a shot on the ground.

Catching Circle

Five players stand in a circle. One throws the ball and then calls a name. That person has to catch the ball. The catcher then calls another name and throws the ball to that player. Introduce a second ball to make the game more challenging.

Benefit: This is a fun way to get your players used to catching the ball.

The Sideways Roll

Two players kneel in an upright position, five yards apart, each between cones about four yards apart. One player rolls the ball about two feet to the side of the other player. The receiver rolls sideways, catches the ball, and rolls back to the upright position. Players take turns rolling the ball to each other. The ball should be rolled to each side in a random pattern.

Benefit: A good introduction to diving for the ball.

Ages 11 to 12

The following drills are for keepers who have a few years of experience.

Shotgun Toss

A player stands ten yards away from the goal, with two or three balls at his feet. The player throws balls at the keeper—high balls, ground balls, balls at the waist, balls to the left and to the right. The object is to loosen up the keeper, rather than to score.

Benefit: This is a good way for a keeper to limber up before a match.

About-Face

The keeper plays between two cones, with teammates on opposite sides, each 15 yards away. The keeper takes a shot from one player, returns the ball, and turns around to take a shot from the other player. The sequence is repeated until the keeper needs a break.

Benefit: The keeper learns how to face a shot without much time to prepare. A good endurance drill, too.

Balls at the Bar

The keeper stands in the goalmouth. A teammate stands about five yards away. The teammate lobs one ball after another toward the upper corners of the net. The keeper backpedals, leaps and catches, backpedals, leaps and deflects, backpedals, leaps and punches.

Benefit: This helps your keeper learn how to defend shots that are over his head.

Defusing the Bomb

A player moves to the side and serves crosses into the goal box. The keeper comes out and catches as many as he can, making the shortest run to the ball while catching it at its highest point. The goalkeeper keeps the body turned toward the center of the field, so if the ball gets free, the keeper is prepared for a shot.

Benefit: This drill helps keepers learn how to come off the line to take away dangerous balls into the box.

Double Barrel

Two players each have a few balls near the top corners of the penalty box. One shoots and the keeper makes the save. As soon as the keeper gives a ready signal, the other player shoots. They take turns shooting until the keeper needs a break.

Benefit: This trains the keeper to recover quickly and be prepared for a series of shots.

Chapter 12

Coaching
a Match

Good coaching will help players get the most from each match. The following guidelines are designed to create a positive game experience for all players.

Game Guidelines

Downsize

For starters, be sure to match the conditions of the game to the age of the players. Please see Table 1-3 for recommendations on the size of the field, goals and ball; the length of the game and the number of players on each side. Following this chart is an important first step in creating a positive game environment for players.

Explain the Rules

Make sure players grasp the fundamentals of play. Arrange ample time for this during practices before the first match. Young players, though, will benefit from a refresher before the first match.

Remind them of the following: Only the keeper can use the hands. Try to put the ball in the opponent's net, and keep it out of your own net.

No pushing is allowed. Do not take the ball from a teammate. Play the ball toward your teammates who can move it toward the other goal. Have fun!

Celebrate Hustle, Effort and Teamwork

Make sure to praise players whenever they do something noteworthy. A long run with the ball, a pass to a teammate, a good save by the keeper—these are examples of plays that merit a compliment. Positive reinforcement makes a player feel good, inspires confidence and builds a desire to play more.

De-emphasize Winning and Losing

Do not keep score, at least in the earlier experiences. At young ages, there is no need to focus on winning and losing. When asked the score by a player, say you don't know, but that you are pleased with the way the team is hustling after the ball.

Be Prepared to Be the Referee

Up through age seven, coaches are often called upon to serve as referees. When that is the case, a coach should have an assistant officiate the match. That allows the coach to focus on managing players, making substitutions and providing encouragement. Whether the coach or the assistant is the referee, make sure that person reviews the laws of the game and can effectively control the match.

Let the kids play. Go easy on the whistle. Call corner kicks, goals kicks and throw-ins.

Playing Time, Positional Play and Restarts

In this section, we focus on three age groups—through age seven, eight to ten, and 11 to 12. For each group, we review three important elements to match play—playing time, positional play and restarts.

Through Age Seven

Playing time

For this age group, equal time for every player should be the rule. Even at this young age, some players will be clearly superior to others.

There may be a temptation to play best players the most. In the interest of fairness, however, make sure that every player plays about the same amount. Try to keep track of who starts each match and make sure that each player is in the starting lineup at least a few times.

The Positions

At this age, there is no need to be concerned about positions. In fact, the field should be small enough that each player can run effectively from one end to the other. Players with a year or two of experience can be lined up in "positions" at the outset. Have some of them play "forward," with an emphasis on the attacking half, and some play "defense," with an emphasis on defending the goal. Over the course of each match, each player should get a chance to play the ball, take part in the attack, and defend. With young players, coaches may have a hard time finding anyone to play keeper. When that happens, it may be best to have each player take a turn in goal.

Restarts

Play throw-ins and goal kicks only; corner kicks need not be introduced at this stage. Demonstrate how to throw the ball during the first few minutes of each game. Give the player a second chance to do it right if necessary. The emphasis should be on learning the proper technique. On goal kicks, move the ball a good eight yards in front of the goal line. Insist that opposing players move back another eight yards or so. This compensates for the lack of foot strength at this age and helps to protect the integrity of the game. Otherwise, the stronger team will pounce on weak goal kicks and launch endless attacks on the goal. Play all balls that go across the end line as goal kicks (no corner kicks). This keeps the game moving and eliminates what is for many young players the somewhat awkward concept of the corner kick.

Ages Eight to Ten

Playing Time

Again, at this age, the emphasis should be on fun and fairness. Each player should get a chance to play an equal amount of the game. At the same time, you may find that some players do not want to play each minute, while others do. When that happens, you can balance your lineup so that every player can play as much as he or she would like, keeping in mind that each player should play at least half of the match.

The Positions

Players ages eight to ten who have a few years of experience should begin to experiment at different positions. Have them play some defense, some midfield, some offense and goalkeeper. Through experimentation, they will develop a better understanding of what it takes to play each position. Over time, most players will hone skills and interests that are best suited to a particular position.

Restarts

Play throw-ins, goal kicks and corner kicks. Demonstrate how to throw the ball during the first few minutes of each game. Give the player a second chance to do it right if necessary. Even at this age, the emphasis should be on learning the proper technique. Many players this age can effectively execute corner kicks, so call them as appropriate.

Ages 11 to 12

Playing Time

At this age, continue to emphasize equal time for each player, especially if the team is playing in a recreational league. However, it may be that certain players always want to be on the field, while others are content to spend considerable time on the sidelines. If this is the case, try to play each player according to the player's wishes.

One point to keep in mind: do not favor any one player—no matter how good that player may be—over everyone else. It will inevitably be recognized by others and will not reflect well upon coach or player.

The Positions

By this age, many players will have three of four years of experience. Some players will have played the same position for much of that time and will want to continue doing so. In those cases, it is best to accommodate the player. At the same time, tell players that they are still developing and that playing different positions will broaden their skills and perspective. Move them around; have them experiment. Let them explore the game from every angle.

This is also an appropriate age range for prospective goalkeepers to begin focusing exclusively on that position, if they are so inclined.

Restarts

This age group should play with goal kicks, corner kicks and direct kicks. At this age, fouls and hand balls become more common. Direct kicks are more frequent and more time should be devoted to them. Players can shoot and pass the ball effectively at this age. When the team has a free kick 30 yards or so from the goal, ask the player with the strongest foot to serve the ball into the box. When the team has a direct free kick just outside the penalty area, instruct the player to shoot. See Chapter 9 for more on restarts.

Working with Parents

Encourage parents to get involved with the team. One parent may be able to manage any phone calls that need to be made to the team (for example, to advise that a game has been postponed due to bad weather). Another may be able to help coach and referee during practices and matches. And a different parent can be assigned to see that snacks are provided at each game.

There may be times when a parent of one player becomes more involved than appropriate. Typically, this happens in one of the following ways.

Parent Says Child Is Not Playing Enough

In recreational play, each player should play roughly the same amount of time. Coaches who follow this rule can tell parents that each player receives about equal time.

Parent Yells Instructions or Criticizes Child During Game

"Pass the ball." "Run over there." "Bad play." "You're not hustling." Young players do not benefit from a chorus of instructions while they are on the playing field. They may become nervous and force their play. Players need to learn to make decisions on their own. Let them decide what to do with the ball. They will learn from every decision they make—both good and bad.

Think of taking kids to the beach. When they team up to build a sandcastle, they make all the decisions on their own. Parents don't stand over them, telling them to "put a tower over here," or to "dig the moat three inches deeper." Parents let them use their imagination. They make the decisions. The same principle should apply on the soccer field.

While parents should refrain from providing instructions or criticisms during the match, they should provide general encouragement. "Nice hustle," "good pass," and "great save" are examples of positive praise that will be well received by players.

Remind parents that the best time to provide input is before or after the game, not during it. The coach can provide constructive comment from the sidelines, and will do so with a light touch.

Parent Says Coach Is Doing Something Wrong

Hear out the parent. Calmly explain the situation. A coach can remind the parent that "I am volunteering my time to coach, and I'm doing the best I can." Do this in an informative, non-confrontational style. If the parent makes a good point, acknowledge it, and thank the parent.

Working with the Referee

For ages five to seven, the coaches of both teams will often be the referees. Take a low-key approach; let them play. At the same time, keep on the lookout for shoving and for intentional hand balls. When a player goes down on the ball, stop play at once. To avoid injury, err on the side of caution. Be prepared to demonstrate throw-ins and goal kicks. And when a call is in doubt, be willing to favor the other team. If both referees take this approach, there will be no disagreements during the game. And do not keep score—even though many of the players will!

With older players, trained referees will officiate matches. Meet with the referee before the match. Make sure the referee's views are understood. Learn, for example, where they want coaches to stand, and when substitutions can be made.

Above all else, treat the referee with respect. Do not yell at the referee. Do not challenge a call during the course of the match. Remember, everything a coach does sets an example for the players. When a coach shows respect for the referee, players will do the same. Calmly discuss disagreements with the referee after the match.

Chapter 13

The 10 Most Important Things a Coach Can Do

Chances are most coaches will not commit everything in this book to memory, or feel they have time to read every word. With that in mind, the following "10 most important things coaches can do" has been compiled. Focusing on these 10 priorities will help one become an effective coach. One will know what to teach and how to teach it, thereby creating a positive learning environment for players.

1. Praise Freely

Be consistently positive with players. Build them up. They need encouragement and praise to feel good about themselves and build confidence in their abilities.

Make sure to spread the praise around. Look to give every player a "pat on the back." Acknowledge kids for hustle, for not giving up, for a good pass, for a strong defensive play. The opportunities are there; take advantage of them.

Most teams have one player who stands out—a skilled, energetic player who makes one superb play after another. Be sure to compliment that player, as too often the best player is overlooked. Every player wants positive feedback from the coach, including the player with the best skills.

Keep expectations in check. Players are just learning the game.

Never criticize a young player for a physical mistake. Each player is trying to do his or her best. No player wants to pass the ball to an opponent, but sometimes this happens. When it does, the player will know of the mistake and need not be told.

Mental mistakes are a different matter. If a player is holding the ball too long, not passing or not hustling, point this out to the player. Be careful, however, to do so in a positive way that will encourage the player to learn. Rather than saying, "Billy, stop hogging the ball," say, "Billy, keep an eye out for teammates. A good pass can be much more effective than dribbling the ball." The player will get the message.

2. Match the Game to the Players

Every action must fit the age of the players. Speak to them in short, punchy sentences. In practice, use drills and games that engage and challenge them. Keep the practices short enough to hold their interest.

Again, be sure to tailor the matches to players. Small players mean small ball, small goals, small field, small sides. This point cannot be overstated! There is nothing more discouraging to a tentative young player than being put on a field 100 yards long with 19 other seven-year-olds. The player will never touch the ball, will be reduced to a spectator, and will lose interest in a hurry.

Instead, put that player in a three versus three game in a box about 20 yards long by ten yards wide. The player will be engaged, will touch the ball often and will begin to develop a relationship with the ball. The player will learn how to make decisions with the ball. Should I dribble, shoot, pass or shield? What direction should I go in? Where can I run so I can receive a pass? Where can I run so I can steal the ball?

3. Get Help

Coaching is hard work. Think of it in three segments—administration, practice and games. No coach, no matter how committed or energetic, can be expected to handle all of the many tasks associated with these three areas. Get help with each one.

Administration

Appoint one parent to handle the many off-the-field details. This includes setting up a roster with players' and parents' names, phone numbers and e-mail addresses, handing out the schedule, setting up a phone chain in the event a practice or game is postponed or cancelled, and setting up a snack schedule so that parents take turns providing refreshments at games.

Practice

Set up a lot of short-sided drills and games. Young players learn best when they engage with the ball. The team can be divided into two groups. With an assistant, that person can watch one group, the coach the other. Each player benefits from receiving praise and constructive feedback throughout the practice.

An assistant can also help set up and break down practice. The assistant may move goals, set up cones or even inflate balls before practice starts.

Games

There are as many as three important tasks for the coach during the game. One is determining who plays when. A second is watching the game and providing encouragement to the players. A third is to referee or help referee the match, at least with very young players.

A coach should not have to do everything. A coach may decide to manage the lineup and substitutions. An assistant can run the sideline and provide support to the players on the field. Yet another could referee the match.

The point is, the coach is better off pulling in one or two reliable people to help manage all the details, both on and off the field. Ideally, find someone who has some background in the sport. But even if the volunteer doesn't know soccer, eagerly accept offers to help as needed. That person can perform many of the tasks mentioned here. The game can be picked up quickly. By mid-season, the person may be able to give some important guidance about individual players and about the team in general.

4. Teach Players the Proper Kicking Technique

It sounds so simple but it's not.
There are still soccer coaches in the United States who encourage their players to kick the ball with their toes. This is not how soccer is

played. Yes, a young player may find that the ball can be kicked a long way with the toes. But ask the player to do it with accuracy and the sham is exposed.

Tell players that the inside and outside of the foot are best for dribbling and short passes. Most young players take quickly to using these parts of the foot.

The harder kick to learn is the kick with the instep. Focus players on pointing the toes toward the ground as the leg comes into the ball. Tell them to kick the ball with the top of the laces. Demonstrate.

Many young players will not point the toe. They will kick the ball with the top of their foot, just above the toes. The ball will not travel far and they will wonder why they can't kick the ball the way their teammates can.

Provide individual instruction as needed. With a ball in hand, stand three yards apart from the player. Drop the ball and kick it out of the air with the instep into the player's hands. Ask the players to do the same. With practice, the player will learn how to use the instep to drive the ball hard and low.

5. Emphasize the Shot

Too many soccer players are afraid to shoot. They worry that their shot will be saved, or worse, sail high or wide. They think that if they shoot but do not score, somehow they have failed. This is true of even the best players at all age levels.

Do not let players fall into this trap. Encourage them to shoot every time they think that have a chance to score. That is the only way they will learn to develop an instinct for the goal and the accuracy that goes with it. When they shoot and miss, congratulate them on creating the opportunity. Never berate a player for a missed shot, except under these circumstances:

- The shot was from an impossible angle
- The shot was from near midfield
- The shooter could have passed to a teammate in a much better position

Spend time in practice on shooting drills. Break up the players into groups of three or four so each player gets several shots on goal. Encourage players to develop the ability to shoot with either foot.

6. Use Soccer to Teach Players about Principles

Many of the principles that apply to soccer apply to life as well. As a coach teaches players the correct way to play soccer, the coach will also be conveying important lessons about life. Thus, when stressing the need for players to work with others, make the broader point that success is rarely accomplished by one person acting alone. Teamwork is critical in soccer, just as it is in life.

Moreover, instill in players the importance of respect – for themselves, their teammates, their coaches, the referee and the opponent. This will carry over into how players treat people in all facets of their lives.

Furthermore, and this may be the most important lesson – teach players to develop an appreciation for fair play. Soccer has rules and every player must abide by them. This, too, will be a good primer for life.

7. Find Time for Each Player

Set aside a few minutes in every practice and every game for individual coaching and instruction. Before each practice, select one, two or perhaps three players to focus on. Think about what to tell each one. Provide a balance between positive input and constructive input. Start with a compliment. Think, too, about an area of the game that each such player should focus on. Be positive. For example, if a player is not hustling back on defense, say, "Bobby, you're making good passes and helping to lead the attack. That's good. At the same time, we really need your support when the other team gets the ball and starts toward our goal. I'd like you to focus on coming back and defending after the ball turns over."

Young players crave attention. By spending a little time with each one, coaches show that they care about the team, yes, but also about each individual on the team. And remember, players look up to coaches and value their word. Always be positive.

8. Be a Humble Winner

There will be times, both in recreation and traveling soccer, when one team is vastly superior to the opponent. It will not take long for this to become apparent. One team may find itself ahead by 3-0 before the fans have settled in their seats.

When this happens, show mercy for the other team. Once the lead becomes insurmountable (say, 5-0), make changes to limit any additional scoring. One way to do so is to play with one fewer player than the opposition. Another is to discreetly instruct your players to use only their left foot. Another is to require a certain number of passes be strung together before a shot can be taken.

The dominant team will still get a good workout. The other team, while demoralized, will not have to walk away on the short end of a 13-0 score. At some point a dominant team will find itself up against an even superior team. They will feel a lot better at the end of the match if the opposing coach shows this kind of consideration for them.

9. Give Players a Voice

Most coaches are more comfortable talking than they are listening. Commit to being good at both.

Make a point to engage players on a regular basis. Open each practice with a review of the previous game. Ask players open-ended questions. "Why did we win?" "What did we do well?" "What can we do better?"

Then let them talk. Players will feel good about the chance to share their opinions with their coach and teammates. Give all players a chance to offer their views. When they make a good point, let them know. Always give a considerate response.

Engage players throughout the practice as well. Once in a while, when a player does something well during a scrimmage, stop the practice. Ask the team what just happened. When Joey says, "Erica knew she couldn't score from that angle so she passed it back to Kevin for a better shot," then two positives have been produced. Erica gets a compliment for her play and Joey is congratulated for his accurate assessment of the play.

Every coach, at every level, can learn something from the players.

10. Keep the Big Picture in Mind

It's only a game. It's only a small part of players' lives. It is not training for the United States National Team.

Yes, make the most of the season. Do whatever can be done to enrich the experience for players. But keep it all in perspective. Players are children who have a lot more to experience than winning at soccer.

Some coaches have unreasonably high expectations of their players. Some traveling team coaches forbid their players from playing other sports. Some even go so far as to tell their players not to play sports during recess because to do so would risk injury.

Young players who are serious about the sport will naturally seek a high level of commitment. That's fine. Encourage them to play as much as is appropriate. That said, the vast majority of young players, no matter how skilled, will want to do other things, too. Let them do so. No young person should be confined by soccer.

Appendix A

Common Questions
and Answers

Here are some of the more common questions that a coach is likely to face, along with answers.

Does my child need cleats or are sneakers okay?

Sneakers may do on a hard, dry field, but rarely over a full season will all games be played on that surface. Cleats are the better option.

Cleats are designed to grip any kind of turf well. There are two kinds of cleats—those with molded studs and those with replaceable "studs" or "screw-ins." Cleats with rubber moldings are best for a dry, hard grass field. They also work best on damp fields. Players up to age 12 can use molded cleats under any conditions.

On wet, soggy fields, older players may find that studded boots work best. These typically have six replaceable studs that screw into the sole—four in the front and two in the back. The studs are longer than molded cleats and therefore sink deeper into soft terrain, providing better traction (see Chapter 2 for more on equipment).

My 12-year-old son is feeling pressure to give up other sports and play soccer year-round. What do you suggest?

What does the player want to do? He should make the decision. If he enjoys other sports, he should continue to play them. Young athletes should have the freedom to experiment. They should not have to specialize, unless they choose to. If the player becomes truly elite, he will likely play on select teams and will play more and more soccer. There may come a time when he has to decide—do I want to devote all my athletic time to soccer or do I want to continue to play two or even three sports? Sometimes this can be a very tough decision. Unless the player is truly exceptional, he may prefer to play several different sports, including soccer. There are people who gave up a lot through their teen years to focus only on soccer (or another sport) only to reach college (or even high school) and never play competitively again.

Of course, it will also depend on the attitude of the coaches involved. Some coaches are very good about tolerating conflicts that arise among two- or three-sport athletes. Others have no tolerance when one of their athletes wants to play another sport. The world would be a better place if high school coaches showed some flexibility and left most of this up to the athletes. Not all do.

Don't soccer players have to play year-round to fulfill their potential?

No. Twenty years ago, traveling teams did not exist in much of the country. Many young players played organized soccer only in the fall, yet they still managed to grow and mature into better players year in and year out. It is true that constant practice can elevate the level of play. But kids and their parents should not feel that young players have to play soccer throughout the year to make significant improvements in their play. This is especially true for kids up to age 13. Past that age, the best players may well want to focus on soccer, and as a result, will end up playing it through much of the year.

How much soccer is too much?

Malcolm Berry, chief executive officer of the English Schools Football Association, observes: "Many young players are unaware that they are damaging their futures by being too successful—too early! Four or five matches each week, resulting in over 100 matches in a season—is exploiting talent and not developing it. We all have a responsibility to protect the young players, encouraging them to spend more time developing skills rather than participating in too many physical and competitive games. Only gradually should the developing skills be transferred to the toughness of the competitive game." Adds Gary Lineker, England's second-leading goal scorer in international play: "We have to cut down the amount of soccer we play, because we get lots of injuries. The quality of the game suffers because players are never fresh." Up to age nine or ten, two sessions a week (one practice, one game) during the season is a good middle ground. Older players can play several times a week but should mix their training to include skill work, match play and physical conditioning. At no age should players log more than three games in a week, and even that is on the heavy side.

My child is much shorter than other players. Is that a detriment?

It can actually be an advantage. Short players can get ahead by using their quickness to elude larger players. Kevin Keegan of England is only five feet, eight inches, but that didn't stop him from becoming one of the greatest goal scorers of all time. Another former English star, Archie Gemmell, is five feet, five inches, yet he was one of the world's top playmakers. American Rick Davis, at five feet, eight inches, became a great player by developing his leg strength. "Since I didn't have great speed or exceptional skills, I needed another weapon. The strength in my legs gave me the ability to win free balls, ward off larger players and distribute the ball effectively." Dynamite can come in small packages!

What should my 12-year-old eat before matches?

The right diet can help players keep their strength up and play better soccer. Foods that contain a large amount of carbohydrate will give players the energy they need to perform at their best. Mike Dickinson, a trainer for the boys' under-15 team in England, says the best energy foods are pasta, potatoes, rice, vegetables, fruit and bread. He says to eat plenty of these foods during the two to three days leading up to the match. He suggests players eat their pre-game meal at least two and a half hours before kick-off. A final tip: eat a banana on game day. Bananas are high in potassium, which helps prevent cramps.

My nine-year-old is clearly superior to her peers. Should she play against older competition?

Yes, as long as the physical differences are not significant. As long as the player can physically compete with older players, she can benefit from doing so. On the other hand, if you put a ten-year-old with 15-year-olds, the player may be able to keep pace technically and tactically, but will be overwhelmed physically.

Would my 12-year-old, who plays on a traveling team, benefit from professional individual instruction?

Chances are he or she can. A number of coaches and camp counselors provide this kind of specialized training. It is best to start with someone the parents and player know and respect; perhaps the child has enjoyed a camp counselor. If no one comes to mind, check with a local soccer club. It may be able to recommend one or two trainers. Interview at least two potential instructors and learn about their background in the sport—playing, coaching, individual training. Seek references and follow up on them. It is also important to focus on what is wanted for the child from the sessions and to communicate that to the instructor right up front, so progress can be effectively measured.

Should boys and girls play together?

Most soccer coaches support coed play up until a certain age. It is difficult to find any drawbacks to boys and girls playing together up through age seven. After that age, many clubs separate girls from boys because of physical differences.

What's the difference between coaching boys and girls?

Many coaches feel that, on balance, girls are easier to coach than boys. Girls listen better, analyze the game more intently, and are eager to accept constructive comments about their play. Boys, on the other hand, are more apt to want to learn by doing. They are not so keen on being pulled aside for a critique, especially after they become teenagers. In addition, girls take the game more personally than boys do. An example: if at halftime of a match a coach told a team of girls that "the team is not running enough," each girl would likely think that she is the one who needs to run more. If a coach said the same thing to a team of boys, each boy would likely think that his teammates better start hustling. These, of course, are generalizations, but it is worthwhile to think about these differences.

How can I learn about summer soccer camps?

Ask people for recommendations. Contact the local soccer association. Scour weekly and daily newspapers for ads. There are many good soccer camps available across the country. Look for camps taught by experienced coaches with a long track record of success. Many young players get hooked on soccer after attending a well-run camp where they receive a lot of attention and get a chance to simply play the game.

My nine-year-old wants to play defense and nothing else. What should I say?

Young players should play all the positions. Suggest she play half the game at defense and a quarter each in midfield and forward. Playing different positions, especially at a young age, helps players develop the full range of soccer skills. A nine-year-old who plays only defense, for example, will have limited opportunities to develop dribbling skills. Playing all the positions also gives young players a better perspective on how the game is played.

My four-year-old wants to play. Is he too young?

Four and five-year olds enjoy kicking a ball. There are mini-camps for this age group, often conducted in a gym. The emphasis should be on fun—put a ball on the floor and let the kids bang it around. Competitive games should not be played at this age.

Should my ten-year-old try out for the traveling team or play recreational soccer?

This can be a difficult decision. Traveling soccer generally requires a greater commitment—for player and parent—than does recreational soccer. There are more practices and more games, more time traveling to and from games and higher costs. There is also a greater emotional commitment in that the pressure to win increases on a traveling team.

Advanced players who want to try out for traveling teams have little to lose. Even if they don't make it, they are free to play recreational soccer. That said, many players—including some exceptional ones—may not want all the responsibility that comes with traveling soccer. They may prefer to stay with the more casual environment of recreational play and leave more time for other pursuits. Tell the child about the differences between the two, and work with the child to make the decision.

Will players who do not play traveling soccer fall behind?

This is a tough question to answer. It is true that players facing top competition tend to become better players for it. Up through age 12, the quality of coaching is most important. An outstanding recreational coach can bring out the best in young players, the level of the competition notwithstanding. As players get older, they are likely to benefit from playing with and against advanced players.

What can a coach do when a match is clearly one-sided?

When a team goes ahead by five or more goals, suggest some changes. At young ages, let the weaker team play with an extra player and consider shortening the game. With kids who've played for a few years, tell them they must pass the ball at least three times in a row before attempting a shot. Another approach is to tell players that they can play the ball only with their weaker foot. Remind players not to gloat about a big lead. This can get them in trouble, especially among older players who are more sensitive to the outcome of a match. After the game, instruct players to congratulate the other team on a game well played.

*There is a player who executes the slide tackle
extraordinarily well. But I worry that this player will
hurt someone or commit a foul in the box. How
can this be controlled without discouraging the player?*

This is a delicate issue. Used well, the slide tackle can be an effective weapon. Defenders, in particular, use it as a last resort in attempting to shut down an opponent's attack on goal. However, a reckless slide tackle can result in injury, a foul and even the expulsion of the offending player.

The rules hold that a slide tackle from behind can warrant a foul and a red card to the offender. Be sure to ban all slide tackling from behind. No exceptions, not even for the player who has the technique down so well that the player gets the ball first even when tackling from behind.

Stress to players that they are better off defending while on their feet. Think how long it takes to get up off the ground and back into playing position. If a player gets past the defender and the only chance left is to slide, make sure it is done so from the side.

A coach may want to ban slide tackling from practices. Young players can easily sustain injury when on the receiving end of a sliding tackle. A mistimed slide may result in a cleat to the ankle, which could sideline a player for weeks. Generally, the slide tackle should be used sparingly until players reach their teen years.

Why should every player play the same amount of time?

Young players should be given every opportunity to develop their skills and enjoy playing the game. Up through age 12, the emphasis should be on learning and playing, not on the final score.

When young teammates play approximately the same amount of time each game, they have a sense that they are contributing their fair share to the team. Young players who spend an inordinate amount of time on the sideline may feel a sense of inferiority that impedes their development and undercuts their self-confidence. Young players who are doing their best, regardless of ability, should not be made to feel that their best is not good enough.

A coach may ask, "But what if the other team insists on keeping its best players on the field when the game is on the line?"

Here's where a distinction can be made between traveling soccer and recreational soccer. A coach of a traveling team may feel compelled to give the strongest players a bit more time on the field during close matches. However, keep track of how much each player plays. The next time the team builds a comfortable lead, make sure to give extra time to the players who sat more during the close games. In the end, every player gets a chance to play a fair share.

As players reach their teenage years, the emphasis on winning grows. It is likely that the more advanced players will play the majority of the game. The less advanced players will accept a lesser role, play recreational soccer or focus their energies elsewhere.

How does one handle a big kid who insists on shielding the ball all the time?

Bigger players may try to use their size to keep possession of the ball. Discourage this practice by stressing the basic tenets behind shielding. This skill should be used to control the ball under pressure. The goal is to ward off the opponent while the player with the ball looks to do something productive with it. The player in possession should be looking to get the ball away from the opponent—either by making a pass to a teammate or by dribbling away into open space.

No player should shield the ball for more than a second or two. Doing so invites other opponents to close in, which nearly always causes the shielding player to lose possession. When a player is holding the ball too long, blow the whistle. Review the principles behind shielding. If the action persists, ask the offending player to keep track of time. The clock starts when the player gets the ball. If after pressure is applied the clock strikes three, blow the whistle and give the ball to the opponent.

Another way to discourage overshielding is to encourage other players to support the player with the ball. Move into space. Call for a pass. Give the teammate an easy way out.

How should a coach treat a player who dogs it in practice?

First, make expectations clear at the first practice. Players are there to learn how to play soccer and to have fun doing it. Tell them each player is to pay attention and to give his or her best at every practice. Misbehavior or lack of effort will not be tolerated.

Most players will be focused on learning and will do their best on a consistent basis. Chances are, however, that there will be one or two players who need special attention. These players may have a short attention span, they may be playing only at the wish of a parent, or they simply may not have an interest in the sport. These young players may be easily distracted and engage in counterproductive activities. Players may chase each other, kick away each other's balls, or jaw at each other while the coach is instructing.

Call the players over. Tell them in private that this behavior will not be tolerated. If it continues, tell the offender(s) to run a lap around the field. This will shame many players into better behavior. If the problem persists, sit the player down for ten minutes during practice. If it continues still, sit the player for the rest of the practice. Contact a parent THAT NIGHT and explain the situation. Expect improved behavior. If it does not happen, contact the league administrator to discuss your alternatives. Other players should not have to put up with the distractions created by a chronically misbehaving player.

A coach may also encounter a player who does not give full effort. Let players know that they are expected to play hard at every practice. Players who misbehave or give half-hearted effort have not earned the right to equal playing time in games.

Dock these players accordingly. Play them about half the time the others play. Tell them why. This is fair punishment and a way to motivate slackers to mend their ways.

Should a player who misses practice be disciplined?

The important point here is to set the rules before the season and make sure players and parents understand them. Most coaches are willing to overlook one or two missed practices during the season.

Some coaches excuse players who miss practice because of a family event, such as traveling on vacation, attending a religious event or attending a birthday party. But when players miss practice to play another sport or pursue another interest, the coach may consider that to be an unexcused absence.

Any player who regularly misses practice for whatever reasons is not showing a reasonable commitment to the team. The coach should address this with the player's parents, making it clear that the player must attend practice if he or she expects to play in the games.

Remember to be fair in applying the rules. The best player on the team must receive the same treatment as every other player.

There are many ways to discipline a player who has missed practice. A common approach is to have the player sit out the first half of the next game. This approach can be used for the first two unexcused absences. Should the player miss another practice, he or she could be asked to sit out the first three quarters of the game.

What should be said to a player who has become angry?

When a player becomes angry, address the situation immediately. The player may erupt at the referee, spar with an opponent, or even argue with a teammate. As soon as it happens, remove the player from the game at the next opportunity. Take the player aside, away from other players or parents. Explain what happened in clear terms. Tell the player that he or she has lost focus. The player's performance has suffered, and therefore the team suffered. This kind of behavior is not fair to the team. Explain that they should focus totally on the game and that any behavior inconsistent with this focus will not be tolerated. If this behavior is repeated, the player will have to spend more time on the bench.

It is critical that players understand at a young age the consequences of losing composure. By stressing this early, players will learn to focus their energy on the game and they will be able to play through any distractions.

Why shouldn't score be kept at young ages?

For the younger players, the emphasis should be entirely on having fun and on fair play. When players are just learning how to play the game, there is no need to be concerned with winning. Coaches who keep score during games involving five, six and seven-year-olds run the risk of causing players on the losing team to develop negative feelings about the sport. Every six-year-old should feel good about every match played.

"I played soccer today." "I had fun." "I kicked the ball several times." "I made some good passes." "I enjoyed being a part of a team." These are the thoughts that should be in the heads of young players when they come off the field. They should not be thinking: "We lost 7–0 today." "We've lost every game this season." "We stink." "I'm no good at soccer." "I think I'll play something else next year."

The kids who score goals at this age don't need a scoreboard to remind them of their feat. They know they scored; they will feel good about it for some time after the final whistle. Let them enjoy their feelings in the privacy of their own minds, rather than broadcasting the score and making the other team feel inferior.

What does one do when no one wants to play goalkeeper?

This is a fairly common situation. Most young players want to be out on the field, running, dribbling, shooting and passing. The thought of standing in front of the goal, often with nothing to do for minutes at a time, is not appealing to most youngsters.

First, emphasize the importance of the position. The keeper is the last line of defense, and therefore plays an important role in the success of the team. Set aside time in practice to engage all players in goalkeeping drills.

Chances are one or two players will "catch on" and decide to give the position a try. Encourage these players; constantly remind them how important they are to the team. Tell them how much their willingness to play the position is appreciated.

An important point—make sure that the keeper also spends time playing on the field. Let's say, for example, that there are two keepers among 12 players on the team. Each plays half the game in goal and half the game on the field. The other ten players split time on the field amongst themselves. This is a reward to the keepers, who are the only players who play the entire game.

If no one on the team wants to play keeper, develop a rotation in which each player on the team splits time evenly in goal. This democratic approach may be the only fair way to resolve the issue.

I'm not able to demonstrate the techniques young players need to learn. What can I do?

Try to find someone who can help at practice. Young soccer players learn from watching others. It is important that they see how to do things, not just hear about them.

Ask the parents if any of them may be able to assist. Once they see there is a need, there is a good chance that one or more will step forward.

If that does not work, ask around to see if an older player can lend his or her time. This could be a player who is two or three years older than the players on your team.

Another option is to ask the local high school coaches if they can help. They can ask their players to lend a hand. Those players may be able to use this time toward a volunteer requirement they have at school. Most high school players would enjoy the chance to be seen as the expert in front of younger players.

What's the difference between playing on grass and playing on artificial turf? What should young players play on?

The vast majority of professional and recreational soccer games are played on grass. A well-kept grass field is ideal. The ball rolls and bounces with a natural, predictable rhythm. On artificial turf, the ball tends to roll faster and bounce more than it does on grass. This can be disruptive to the flow of the game, especially for players who are not used to playing on turf. Turf also tends to be harder than grass, leading to more injuries when players go down. Grass is the preferred surface by the overwhelming majority of the global soccer community. Young players should play on grass as much as possible.

Appendix B

Ten Quick Tips

1. Tie the knot in the right spot!

Tell players to put the knot in their shoelaces on the part of the foot they use least. For example, if the player tends to favor the outside of the foot when dribbling, then the knot should be tied on the inside of the shoe. The knot won't be in the way of the ball.

2. Eat to win!

Players can keep their strength up and play better soccer by sticking to a healthy diet. Foods that contain a large amount of carbohydrates will give players the energy they need to perform at their best. Pasta, potatoes, rice, vegetables, fruit and bread are good energy foods. Encourage players to eat plenty of these foods during the two or three days before a game.

One more tip: Tell players to eat their pre-game meal at least two and a half hours before kick-off.

3. Keep your game grounded!

Encourage players to play the ball on the ground. A pass on the ground is easy for the receiver to control. In fact, the ball can be first-timed or nudged into space. A ball coming in off the ground must be controlled first. It takes a second or so to bring a ball to the ground—precious time when an opponent is closing in.

4. Keep a foot on the ball.

Take advantage of every opportunity to help players develop a feel for the ball with their weaker foot. Tell them that they should never sit on their ball. When players gather at the start and end of each practice, ask them to stand with their natural foot on the ground and the other foot on top of the ball. This will help build a relationship between their weaker foot and the ball. Over time, this simple approach will help players learn to be more comfortable with their weaker foot.

5. Use contests to motivate players.

Young players like to create "personal bests." Keep this in mind during practices. When players are in individual drills, ask them to keep track of their best performance. For example, if the kids are playing "foot boxing" to warm up, ask them to count the number of times they tap the ball in 15 seconds. Give them four or fives chances to beat their first score. They will be motivated to do so!

Do the same when players are doing drills in pairs. Some examples: how many times can they head the ball back and forth before it hits the ground? How many times in a row can they thread passes between two cones?

6. Keep a pump handy at all times.

At every practice one normally finds at least one ball lacking air. A $5 investment in a ball pump will pay for itself many times over. During the ten minutes before practice, inspect each ball and inflate as needed. Pump the balls so they are firm but not rock-hard. There should be a little give in the ball after it has been pumped. This is important, especially for younger players who will not want to head a ball that has no give to it.

Players will appreciate this service. A deflated or overinflated ball will not travel as it should. Players should have a properly inflated ball that flies true.

7. Take players to see older players.

Try to arrange a "field trip" to a high school, college or professional game in the area. Chances are one can find such a match without having to look too hard or drive too far.

Players will benefit in many ways. First, it is a chance for players to get to know each other better. Building camaraderie is important, particularly if the roster stays relatively constant season in and season out.

Second, young players learn by watching others perform. Players will see soccer in a more advanced form—elegant dribbling, effective passing and a lot of running. They will take a few mental notes and begin to experiment on their own. They will be motivated to learn new skills and become better players.

8. Hold your child to a slightly higher standard when you're the coach.

Chances are good that the coach will have a son or daughter on the team. This child should be treated just as every other player. The child should receive the same amount of playing time as other players. The child should be singled out for praise at practice in the same manner other players are.

It's human nature; there will likely be one or two parents watching to see if the "coach's kid" receives special treatment. Give these folks nothing to work with; in fact, hold the child to an ever so slightly higher standard. Don't set the standard so high that it is unfair (as the child will feel unjustly treated) but high enough that it is clear to other parents that there is no favoritism. Remember, a coaching parent can make up for any tiny deficit with a few extra words of praise on the ride home.

9. Every player is a captain.

Young players like to be leaders. Give each player on the team a chance to be captain during the season. Depending on the number of games played, there can be solo captains, co-captains or tri-captains for each match. This can be done alphabetically to head off any concerns about favoritism.

It can be thrilling to hear: "Hey Mom and Dad, I was team captain today."

10. Celebrate the season!

After the last game, invite players and their parents over for pizza and soda or meet at a restaurant.

Thank the players for the effort they gave. If time and resources allow, make up certificates honoring each player on the team. Personalize each one, to recognize a special attribute of each player. "Hustle Award," "Tough Tackler Award," "Fancy Footwork Award," the list goes on.

Thank the parents for their help. Everyone likes to be recognized for the good deeds they do.

Ask for feedback. How did the season go? What did people like? What could have been done better? It's a great opportunity to learn.

Glossary

Attacking: Aggressively moving the ball forward into scoring position.

Ballwatching: When a player stands and watches the ball instead of moving into space.

Back heel pass: A pass made with the heel to a trailing teammate.

Banana kick: A ball kicked with the inside or outside of the foot that curves through the air.

Bicycle kick (overhead kick): When a player jumps, leans backward, kicks one leg overhead and then strikes the ball with the second leg before landing on one's back.

Block tackle: Tackling the opponent head-on to gain possession.

Cap: What players receive each time a game is played for their national team.

Caution: A warning given by the referee to a player who argues too much or repeatedly commits fouls.

Chip (wedge): A shot lobbed high in the air to avoid a defender or the keeper.

Clearing: Moving the ball away from the front of the goal that is being defended.

Controlling: To settle a moving ball. Also called collecting or receiving.

Corner kick: A kick awarded to the attacking team from a corner of the field after the ball has been put over the end line by the defense.

Crossing pass: A pass sent into the center of the field from the flank.

Crossbar: The bar connecting the two goalposts.

Covering: Guarding or marking an opponent.

Direct kick: A shot that may be sent directly into the goal without having to touch another teammate first.

Dangerous play: An infraction called against a player who endangers other players. The most common dangerous play is a high kick made in proximity to other players.

Dribbling: Moving the ball with a series of short kicks.

Drop ball: When the referee drops a ball between two players. The ball must hit the ground before it can be played. Used to restart play after an injury or after a ball goes out of play simultaneously off of two opposing players.

FIFA: Soccer's world governing body, based in Geneva, Switzerland. Stands for the Federation Internationale Des Football Associations.

Far post: The goal post farthest from the ball.

Feint: Disguising the direction you intend to take to deceive the opponent.

Flank: Along the sidelines, where the wings play.

Follow-through: The distance your foot travels after you've kicked the ball.

Formation: How a team aligns its players (4-4-2 means four defenders, four midfielders and two forwards).

Forward: Front line player who leads the offense.

Foul: An action that breaks the rules, such as tripping or obstructing the opponent.

Free kick: A kick awarded to the other team after a foul is committed.

Give and go: When a player passes the ball and runs to open space for a return pass. Called a wall pass.

Goal area: The box immediately in front of the goal, six yards by 18 yards on a regulation field.

Goalkeeper: The last line of defense. The keeper can use his hands inside the penalty box (18 yards by 44 yards on a regulation field).

Goal kick: The kick a team makes from its six-yard line after the ball has gone over the end line last touched by the attacking team.

Goal mouth: The area right in front of the goal.

Goalposts: The uprights of the goal, eight feet high and 24 feet apart on a regulation pitch.

Goal side: The position taken by a defender when playing between the attacker and the defender's goal.

Half-volley: Kicking a ball just after it has struck the ground.

Hand ball: A foul called when a player touches the ball with any part of the arm, resulting in a free kick for the opponent.

Heading: Directing the ball with the forehead.

Indirect kick: A free kick that must touch another player before it can go into the goal.

Instep: The hardest part of the foot, along the shoelaces. Used for shots and long, hard passes.

Inswinger: A ball that swerves toward the goal, after a kick made with the inside or outside of the foot (often used to describe a corner kick).

Jockeying: Moving to stay one yard in front of the player with the ball, slowing him down.

Kick-off. The kick that starts a game or resumes it after a goal is scored. The ball must be played forward.

Linesman: Official who assists the referee. One is on each side of the field.

Man-on: A warning shouted to a teammate who is closely marked but may not know it.

Midfielder: A player who plays behind the forwards and in front of the defenders.

Near post: The goal post nearest the ball.

Nutmeg: The act of slipping the ball through the opponent's legs.

Obstruction: A foul committed when a player jumps into the path of an opponent to keep the opponent from playing the ball.

Offside: A rule that any attacking player must have two defenders, including the keeper, between the player and the goal when the ball is passed to the player by a teammate. The rule does not apply when the player in question is on their own half of the field when the ball is kicked.

One-time, or one-touch: To play the ball without controlling it first.

Open space: A clear area on the field where a player can run to receive the ball.

Overlap: An aggressive run, usually made by a defender, into the attacking zone on the side of the field away from the ball.

Penalty area: The box in front of each goal, 18 yards long by 44 yards wide on a regulation field. The keeper can use his hands in this area only. When the defense commits a hand-ball or a foul in this area, it results in a penalty kick.

Penalty kick: A shot awarded to the attacking team after a deliberate hand ball or foul is committed in the penalty area. The shot is taken 12 yards away from the goal. The keeper's feet must be on the end line until the ball is struck.

Pill: A shot moving so fast that it looks like the size of an aspirin tablet to the goalkeeper.

Pitch: Another term for a soccer field.

Punt: When the keeper drops the ball and kicks it out of the air or just after it hits the ground.

Push up: To run up into the attacking end of the field.

Red card: Issued by the referee against a player who has committed a flagrant foul or abused the referee. The player is expelled and may not be replaced.

Referee: The official in charge. Assisted by two linesmen.

Restart: Used to describe any situation when the game begins or starts again. The start of the game, the start of the second half, throw-ins, goal kicks, free kicks and corner kicks are all restarts. Also called "dead ball" situations.

Scissors kick: A kick made on a ball coming to a player from the side. The player jumps, extends one leg forward toward the target and then strikes the ball with the second leg.

Set piece: Throw-ins, corner kicks, goals kicks and free kicks.

Shielding: Maintaining possession of the ball by keeping the body between the ball and the opponent.

Show: The act of running into space to give a teammate a target.

Sitter: A ball sitting in front of the goal that should be an easy score.

Sliding tackle: When a player slides in with one foot to jar the ball free from an opponent.

Stopper: The player at the top of the defensive diamond. The player marks the other team's top scoring threat.

Striker: A forward who plays toward the middle of the field.

Strip: Another word for uniform.

Sweeper: The player right in front of the keeper. The player usually has no man-to-man responsibilities and instead "sweeps up" for the other defenders.

Tackling: The act of taking the ball from the opponent.

Take on: To challenge an opponent by dribbling at the opponent.

Throw-in: How the ball is put into play after it crosses the sideline. The throw is awarded to the team that did not put the ball out of play. The arms are brought back over the head and the ball is released as the arms come over the head. Feet must remain on the ground.

Touchline: The sideline or the end line.

US Soccer: America's governing body, based in Chicago.

Volley: Kicking the ball while it is in the air.

Wall: A group of players standing side by side to protect the goal from a free kick.

Wall pass: A pass made to a teammate who returns the ball to the passer. Actually two passes.

Wing: A forward playing on the flank.

Wingback: A defender playing on the outside.

World Cup: A tournament held every four years to determine the best team in the world.

Yellow card: Issued by the referee against a player who has committed an infraction. Any player assessed two yellow cards is expelled from the game and may not be replaced.

Index